WORDS FROM WILLS

and other probate records

A GLOSSARY

Stuart A. Raymond

BALH

BRITISH ASSOCIATION
FOR LOCAL HISTORY

Words from Wills and other probate records
a Glossary

First edition published 2004 by the Federation of Family History Societies

This edition published by the British Association for Local History 2025
c/o Moore Insight, St James House
Vicar Lane, Sheffield S1 2EX
01625 664524
admin@balh.org.uk

BALH
BRITISH ASSOCIATION
FOR LOCAL HISTORY

Typeset in ITC New Baskerville by John Chandler

ISBN 978-0-948140-07-5

The front cover illustration is a detail from Wiltshire & Swindon Archives, P3/M/257, with thanks to Wiltshire Council and Salisbury Diocese.

Contents

Introduction

Wills and other probate records of the sixteenth to eighteenth centuries are vital sources for family and local historians, and have been used for a wide variety of purposes by modern researchers. They provide genealogists with much information on particular families, they enable local historians to re-construct the culture of the people who wrote them, and they give the basic data from which studies can be made of topics as diverse as furniture, literacy, and agriculture. The words used in them are, however, often no longer used in modern English, and may be difficult to understand for newcomers to historical research. Andirons, beres, and winding sheets were all very familiar items to our seventeenth-century ancestors, but the average person today would have no idea what they were.

The purpose of this book is to provide definitions for words commonly found in early modern probate records. It is based on a wide range of published collections of probate records, listed below. The glossaries in all of the editions listed have been compared and contrasted with each other, and with a number of specialist dictionaries (also listed below); the definitions given derive from this process. Where a word is likely to be localised, I have indicated the county in which it has been found, using the Chapman county code system of abbreviations, detailed below. Such indications are intended as questions rather than authoritative statements.

Spelling during the period covered by this glossary was far from standardised. The same word could be spelt in many different ways. If an attempt were made to list all the variant spellings, the result would be a book twice as long as the present one. I have generally chosen that spelling which most closely corresponds to present-day usage. I have also tended to ignore the frequent addition of -e and -te suffixes to the ends of words, and the common substitution of y for i and e and vice versa, of c for t or s, f for v, etc. Variant spellings which are obvious, e.g. cownterfeit for counterfeit, truckel for truckle, trenchar for trencher, have not been listed. If you come across a word which seems not to be listed here, say it and then work out how you would spell it; you may well then be able to identify a definition. I have included a few variant spellings which might not be obvious, or which might be considered to be different words, perhaps influenced by dialect, e.g. cobberd for cob iron. I have not included definitions for words still in common use, except where their meanings have changed.

The words defined are arranged alphabetically, word by word. Where they consist of two words which are sometimes joined together, I have separated them, e.g. cap case, not capcase. Definitions for words which have several distinct meanings are numbered, so that they can be cross-referenced. Words which are defined elsewhere in the text are marked with an asterisk, and with a number if appropriate.

This glossary is confined to words used in probate records, and to their meanings in that context. Many other meanings are given in the *Oxford English dictionary*, and in Wright's *English dialect dictionary*, both of which have been checked for the words defined here.

The list of published probate records given below only includes those which have been used in compiling this glossary. It is not intended to be comprehensive, although it does include most record society editions containing glossaries. Many other works on probate records are listed in Gibson, Jeremy, & Raymond, Stuart A. *Probate Jurisdictions: Where to look for Wills* (6th ed. Family History Partnership, 2016), in my *English genealogy: a bibliography* (3rd ed., F.F.H.S., 1996), and in the county volumes of my British genealogical library guides. For a detailed guide to probate records, see my *The Wills of our Ancestors* (Pen & Sword, 2012).

Finally, a word of warning. Words used in probate records, and, indeed, in all historical records, must be understood in the light of their context. Words can and do have different meanings in different contexts. A case in point is the word 'horse'. Three different definitions are offered below; a fourth meaning is not given because it is still in common use today. The researcher may need to give some thought to which meaning is intended. It is obviously important to avoid confusing a beast used for riding with a frame for drying clothes, or with trestles for a table. The context, however, will usually make it clear which is intended: riding beasts are most likely to be listed in inventories with other animals; trestles are likely to be with their associated table boards[1].

Acknowledgements

I have been gratified by the reception accorded to this book, and by the fact that a second edition has proved necessary. This edition incorporates information from a number of editions of probate records published since 2004. The original edition was typed by Cynthia Hanson; this edition has been seen through the press by John Chandler. My thanks go to them, and to the officers of the British Association for Local History, the publishers. The book began as the glossary I wrote for my Adelaide University M.A. thesis (see p. 6), and the supervisor of that thesis, Professor Wilfrid Prest, also deserves thanks.

Stuart A. Raymond

---

1. For a full discussion of words and their contexts, see: Trinder, Barrie. 'The wooden horse in the cellar: words and their contexts in Shropshire probate inventories', in Arkell, Tom, Evans, Nesta, & Goose, Nigel, eds. *When death do us part: understanding and interpreting the probate records of early modern England.* Oxford: Leopards Head Press, 2000, pp.268-84.

Bibliography

Dictionaries

SIMPSON, J.A., & WEINER, E.S.C. *The Oxford English dictionary.* 2nd ed. 20 vols. Oxford: Clarendon Press, 1989.

HALLIWELL, JAMES ORCHARD. *A dictionary of archaic and provincial words, obsolete phrases, proverbs, and ancient customs from the fourteenth century.* 10th ed. 2 vols. John Russell Smith, 1887.

BRISTOW, JOY. *The local historian's glossary and vade mecum.* 2nd ed. Nottingham: Dept. of Adult Education, University of Nottingham, 1994.

WRIGHT, JOSEPH, ed. *The English dialect dictionary, being the complete vocabulary of all dialect words still in use, or known to have been in use, during the last two hundred years.* 6 vols. Henry Frowde, 1898-1905.

REDMONDS, GEORGE. *The Yorkshire historical dictionary: A glossary of Yorkshire words, 1120 – c.1900,* ed. Alexandra Medcalf. 2 vols. Yorkshire Archaeological & Hisotircal Society Record series 165-6. 2021.

Collected Editions

Bedfordshire

McGREGOR, MARGARET, ed. *Bedfordshire wills proved in the Prerogative Court of Canterbury, 1383-1548.* Publications of the Bedfordshire Historical Record Society, 58. 1979.

BELL, PATRICIA, ed. *Bedfordshire wills, 1480-1519.* Publications of the Bedfordshire Historical Record Society, 45. 1966.

BELL, PATRICIA L., ed. *Bedfordshire wills 1484-1533.* Publications of the Bedfordshire Historical Record Society, 76. 1997.

TEARLE, BARBARA, ed. *Bedfordshire probate inventories before 1660.* Bedfordshire Historical Record Society, 98. 2024.

COLLETT-WHITE, JAMES. *Inventories of Bedfordshire country houses 1714-1830.* Publications of the Bedfordshire Historical Society, 74. 1995.

Buckinghamshire

REED, MICHAEL, ed. *Buckinghamshire probate inventories 1661-1714.* Buckinghamshire Record Society, 24. 1988.

NOY, DAVID, & ROBINSON, LYN, eds. *Chetwode Wills and Disputes, 1538-1857.* Buckinghamshire Record Society, 41. 2022.

LEWINGTON, HONOR, ed. *Stoke Mandeville Wills and Inventories, 1552-1853. Buckinghamshire* Record Society, 38. 2018.

Cheshire

GROVES, JILL, ed. *Bowdon wills: wills and probate inventories from a Cheshire township.* 3 vols. Sale: Northern Writers Advisory Service, 1997. Pt.1. 1600-1650. Pt.2. 1651-1689. Pt.3. 1690-1760.

PIXTON, PAUL B., ed. *Wrenbury Wills and Inventories, 1542-1661.* Lancashire & Cheshire Record Society, 144. 2009.

Cornwall

ORME, NICHOLAS, ed. *Cornish wills, 1342-1540.* Devon & Cornwall Record Society, New series 50. 2007.

RAYMOND, S.A. *Seventeenth-century Week St. Mary, Cornwall, including an edition of the probate records 1598 to 1699.* M.A. thesis, University of Adelaide, 1988.

Derbyshire

MILWARD, ROSEMARY. *A glossary of household, farming and trade terms from probate inventories.* 2nd ed. Occasional paper, 1. Derbyshire Record Society, 1983.

Devon

CASH, MARGARET, ed. *Devon inventories of the sixteenth and seventeenth centuries.* Devon and Cornwall Record Society, new series, 11. 1966.

CROCKER, JANNINE, ed. *Elizabethan Inventories and Wills of the Exeter Orphans' Court.* Devon & Cornwall Record Society, new series, 56-7. 2013-14.

WYATT, PETER, ed. *The Uffculme wills and inventories, 16th to 18th centuries.* Devon and Cornwall Record Society, new series, 40. 1997.

Dorset

MACHIN, R., ed. *Probate inventories and manorial excepts of Chetnole, Leigh and Yetminster.* [Bristol]: Dept. of Extra-Mural Studies, University of Bristol, 1976.

Durham

ATKINSON, J.A., et al, eds. *Darlington wills and inventories, 1600-1625.* Surtees Society, 201. 1993.

BRIGGS. JOAN, et al, eds. *Sunderland Wills and Inventories, 1601-1650.* Surtees Society, 214. 2010.

BRIGGS. JOAN, et al, eds. *Sunderland Wills and Inventories, 1651-1675.* Surtees Society, 224. 2020.

Gloucestershire and Bristol

LANG, SHEILA, & McGREGOR, MARGARET, eds. *Tudor wills proved in Bristol, 1546-1603.* Bristol Record Society publication, 44. 1993.

SALE, A.J.H., ed. *Cheltenham probate records, 1660-1740.* Gloucestershire record series, 12. Bristol and Gloucestershire Archaeological Society, 1999.

MOORE, JOHN S., ed. *The goods and chattels of our forefathers: Frampton Cotterell and district probate inventories, 1539-1804.* Phillimore & Co., 1976.

Hampshire

ROBERTS, EDWARD, & PARKER, KAREN, eds. *Southampton probate inventories 1447-1575.* 2 vols. Southampton records series, 34-35. 1992.

Hertfordshire

MUNBY, LIONEL M., ed. *Life & death in Kings Langley: wills and inventories, 1498-1659.* Kings Langley: Kings Langley Local History & Museum Society, 1981.

PENWARDEN, JILL & MUSSETT, MAUREEN, eds. *Where there's a Will, there's a Story: Kings Langley Wills and Inventories 1660-1800.* Kings Langley Local History Society, 2004.

HOWE, PAT, & HARRIS, JANE, eds. *Wills, Inventories, and Probate Accounts from St Albans, 1600-1615.* Hertfordshire Record Publication 32. Hertfordshire Record Society, 2019.

Lancashire
PHILLIPS, C.B., & SMITH, J.H., eds. *Stockport probate records, 1620-1650.* Record Society of Lancashire and Cheshire, 131. 1992.

Lincolnshire See also Yorkshire
FOSTER, C.W., ed. *Lincoln wills registered in the District Probate Registry at Lincoln, volume II: A.D. 1505 to May 1530.* Publications of the Lincoln Record Society, 10. 1918. Covers the whole county, not just Lincoln.

AMBLER, R.W., WATKINSON, B., & WATKINSON, L.A. *Farmers and fishermen: the probate inventories of the ancient parish of Clee, South Humberside, 1536-1742.* Studies in regional and local history, 4. Hull: University of Hull School of Adult and Continuing Education, 1987.

JOHNSTONE, J.A., ed. *Probate inventories of Lincoln citizens, 1661-1714.* Publications of the Lincoln Record Society, 80. 1991.

NEAVE, DAVID, ed. *Winteringham 1650-1760: life and work in a North Lincolnshire village, illustrated by probate inventories.* [Winteringham]: Winteringham W.E.A. Branch, 1984.

Norfolk
WILSON, J.H., ed. *Wymondham inventories.* Creative history from East Anglian sources, 1. Norwich: Centre of East Anglian Studies, 1993.

Northamptonshire
EDWARDS, DOROTHY, et al, eds. *Early Northampton Wills preserved in Norfolk Record Office.* Northamptonshire Record Society, 42. 2005.

Nottinghamshire
KENNEDY, P.A., ed. *Nottinghamshire household inventories.* Thoroton Society record series, 22. 1963.

PERKINS, ELIZABETH R., ed. *Village life from wills & inventories: Clayworth parish, 1670-1710.* Record series, 1. Nottingham: University of Nottingham Centre for Local History, 1979.

Oxfordshire
HAVINDEN, M.A., ed. *Household and farm inventories in Oxfordshire, 1550-1590.* Oxfordshire Record Society, 44. 1965. Also published as Historical Manuscripts Commission joint publication, 10.

BRINKWORTH, E.R.C., & GIBSON, J.S.W., eds. *Banbury wills and inventories, part one: 1591-1620.* Banbury Historical Society, 13. 1985.

Shropshire
TRINDER, BARRIE, & COX, NANCY, eds. *Miners & mariners of the Severn Gorge: probate inventories for Benthall, Broseley, Little Wenlock, and Madeley, 1660-1764.* Chichester: Phillimore, 2000.

TRINDER, BARRIE, & COX, JEFF, eds. *Yeomen and colliers in Telford: probate inventories for Dawley, Lilleshall, Wellington and Wrockwardine, 1660-1750.* Chichester: Phillimore & Co., 1980.

Suffolk
NORTHEAST, PETER, ed. *Wills of the Archdeaconry of Sudbury 1439-1474: Wills from the Register Baldwyne, part 1: 1439-1461.* Suffolk Records Society 44. 2010.

EVANS, NESTA, ed. *The wills of the Archdeaconry of Sudbury 1630-1635.* Suffolk

Records Society, 29. 1987.

ALLEN, MARION, ed. *Wills of the Archdeaconry of Suffolk, 1620-1624.* Suffolk Records Society, 31. 1989.

ALLEN, MARION E., ed. *Wills of the Archdeaconry of Suffolk, 1627-1628.* Suffolk Records Society, 58. 2015.

Surrey

HERRIDGE, D.M., ed. *Surrey Probate Inventories1558-1603.* Surrey Record Society, 39. 2005.

Sussex

HUGHES, ANNABELLE, ed. *Sussex Clergy Inventories, 1600-1750.* Sussex Record Society, 91. 1991.

Warwickshire

HOLT, RICHARD, INGRAM, JANET, & JARMAN, JOHN. *Birmingham wills and inventories, 1551-1600.* Birmingham: University of Birmingham Dept. of Extra-mural Studies, 1985.

UPTON, ANTHONY A., ed. *Foleshill probate wills and inventories, 1535-1599.* Foleshill pamphlets, 4. Lighthorne: the author, 1993.

ALCOCK, N.W. *People at home: living in a Warwickshire village, 1500-1800.* Chichester: Phillimore, 1993. Includes inventories for Stoneleigh.

Stratford-upon-Avon inventories I. 1538-1625: glossary. Publications of the Dugdale Society, 29, [supplement]. 2002.

Wiltshire

WILLIAMS, LORELEI, & THOMSON, SALLY, eds. *Marlborough probate inventories, 1591-1775.* Wiltshire Record Society, 59. 2007.

Worcestershire

WANKLYN, MALCOLM, ed. *Inventories of Worcestershire landed gentry, 1537-1786.* Worcestershire Historical Society, new series, 16. 1998.

ROPER, JOHN S., ed. *Dudley probate inventories, 1544-1603.* Dudley: [J.S.Roper], 1965-6.

DYER, A. D., ed. `Probate inventories of Worcester tradesmen, 1545-1614', in *Miscellanea II.* Worcestershire Historical Society, new series, 5. 1967, 1-67.

Yorkshire

NEEDHAM, SUE. *A glossary for East Yorkshire and North Lincolnshire probate inventories.* Studies in regional and local history, 3. Hull: University of Hull Dept. of Adult Education, 1984.

BREARS, PETER C. D., ed. *Yorkshire probate inventories, 1542-1689.* Yorkshire Archaeological Society record series, 134. 1972.

THWAITE, HARTLEY, ed. *Abstracts of Abbotside wills 1552-1688.* Yorkshire Archaeological Society record series, 130. 1968.

KIRK, G. E., ed. `Some documents of Barnoldswick manor court of probate', in WHITING, C. E., ed. *Miscellanea vol. VI.* Yorkshire Archaeological Society record series, 118. 1953, 53-84.

EDWARDS, DOROTHY, & NEWMAN, CHRISTINE M., eds. *Northallerton wills and Inventories, 1666-1719.* Surtees Society 220. 2016.

BERRY, ELIZABETH K., ed. *Swaledale wills and inventories 1522-1600.* Yorkshire Archaeological Society record series, 152. 1998.

Chapman County Codes

The codes listed below have been used to indicate the counties in which particular words have been found in probate records. They have been used sparingly, and are provided merely as suggestions that the words concerned may be confined to a particular county or region. Such suggestions are not to be regarded as authoritative. Only the codes for pre-1974 English counties are listed here.

BDF	Bedfordshire	LND	London
BKM	Buckinghamshire	MDX	Middlesex
BRK	Berkshire	MON	Monmouthshire
CAM	Cambridgeshire	NBL	Northumberland
CHS	Cheshire	NFK	Norfolk
CON	Cornwall	NTH	Northamptonshire
CUL	Cumberland	NTT	Nottinghamshire
DBY	Derbyshire	OXF	Oxfordshire
DEV	Devon	RUT	Rutland
DOR	Dorset	SAL	Shropshire
DUR	Durham	SFK	Suffolk
ESS	Essex	SOM	Somerset
GLS	Gloucestershire	SRK	Sark
HAM	Hampshire	SRY	Surrey
HEF	Herefordshire	SSX	Sussex
HRT	Hertfordshire	STS	Staffordshire
HUN	Huntingdonshire	WAR	Warwickshire
KEN	Kent	WES	Westmorland
LAN	Lancashire	WIL	Wiltshire
LEI	Leicestershire	WOR	Worcestershire
LIN	Lincolnshire	YKS	Yorkshire

GLOSSARY

Abb
Short-stapled wool of a particular quality, usually from the belly of the fleece.

Acacia
Juice of the acacia tree, used as a drug.

Accates
Victuals, purchased provisions. (Dby)

Accompt
Account

Accoucheur
Male midwife.

Advowry
Protector or patron, especially a patron saint, an advocate in heaven.

Adze
Tool similar to an axe, with the blade at right angles to the handle, for straightening and smoothing wood surfaces; particularly used by *coopers.

Afterleaze
Herbage remaining after the hay harvest.

Agistment
The feeding of animals in a park, forest, or other pasture, for a stipulated price.

Aglets
Metal decorations used at the end of laces to prevent them fraying; metal toys or spangles used for fastening garments together, e.g. the sleeves. Also used for the laces themselves.

Agnus Dei
A cake of wax stamped with the figure of the Lamb of God, bearing a cross or flag, perhaps blessed by the Pope.

Alb
A priest's white vestment or tunic, reaching to the feet.

Alchemy
Any metal that imitates gold, e.g. brass.

Alcuin
Antimony (Sal)

Ale Coste
A vessel for ale holding nine gallons.

Ale Stool
Stand for a cask of ale.

Alegar
Sour ale; malt vinegar.

Alembic
*Limbeck.

Alexanders
An umbelliferous plant.

Algars
*Hangings. (War)

Alias
An alternative or assumed name.

Alkanet
A red dye obtained from the roots of the anchusa.

Allamode, Allmood
A thin, light, glossy black silk. (Lin)

Allcamy Spown
Spoon treated with an alloy to make it resemble gold or silver.

Almain Rivets
Light armour, made flexible by overlapping plates on sliding rivets. First used in Germany, i.e. aleman in Old French.

Almery, Almorie
*Aumbry.

Aloe
Bitter tasting purgative drug made from the juice of plants of the genus Aloe.

Altarage
The revenue arising from *oblations at an altar.

Althæ Syrup
A syrup obtained from the marsh mallow plant, used medicinally.

Alum
Potassium aluminium sulphate, used as a mordant in preparing cloth for dyeing, and also in tanning; also used for curing bacon and sizing paper.

Alum Stone
Stone trough for steeping skins in alum.

Alur

A gallery, balcony, or covered walkway.

Ameld

Enamelled.

Amice

White square of linen worn around the head and neck by priests when celebrating mass.

Amortize

To alienate in *mortmain, i.e. to convey property to a corporation (usually ecclesiastical) in perpetuity.

Ancress

Anchoress: a female hermit or nun.

Andier Dog

*Andiron.

Andiron

1.   A horizontal iron bar, supported by a short foot at one end, and an upright pillar or support, usually ornamental, at the other. A pair of these were placed at either side of the hearth, to support logs. Air flowed under them to promote burning. The uprights may also have hooks for pots etc., to hang above the fire, or may support a spit. Distinguished from the simple *dog iron by the ornamental front end.

2.   A pair of movable iron plates to contract the fire grate.

Angel, Angel Noble

Gold coin, introduced in 1465, portraying the Archangel Michael standing on and spearing the dragon; worth between 6s. 8d. and 10s. Last coined by Charles I. This coin was presented to those touched for the `King's evil'.

Angel, Angelica Water

Perfume made from the herb angelica.

Angelet

Gold coin worth half an *Angel.

Anime

A cuirass or breastplate, of Italian origin, constructed of plates overlapping in such a way as to allow comparatively flexible movement.

Anker

1. A measure of wine and spirits, varying by locality, but about four gallons in Dorset; a cask of that capacity.

2. Anchor.

Anoil

To anoint with oil, give extreme unction to the dying.

Antic

Grotesque, fantastic, or incongruous.

Antiphonary

Book containing a collection of antiphons, i.e. short sentences sung alternately by different singers.

Apern

Apron, napery ware.

Apery, Aperyware

*Napery.

Apothecary

Druggist.

Apparel, Appill

Personal clothing.

Apparitor

The servant, attendant, or official messenger of a civil or ecclesiastical court.

Apple Grate, Iron, Roaster

Iron implement for roasting apples over an open fire.

Apple Mill

*Cider Mill.

Apple Wring

Press for crushing apples to make cider. (Dev)

Appraiser

The valuer/compiler of a probate inventory.

Appurtenances

Minor rights or properties belonging to a house or land, and passing with it.

Aqua Coelestis

Alcoholic drink, perhaps made of brandy.

Aqua Fortis

*Strong Waters.

Aqua Vitae

Alcoholic spirits, e.g. brandy, whisky; from the Latin for `water of life'.

Arbor

Trelliswork to train plants over.

Archil

A species of lichen, from which is produced a violet dye, giving a blue wash for walls.

Arders

Ploughing and manuring; the state

of being ploughed and manured; the value of land ploughed up.

Arfarrian
*Orpharion.

Argil
1. Clay, especially potter's clay.
2. *Alum.

Argol
Crude bitartrate of potassium, deposited by fermented wine on the sides of barrels as a hard crust, which becomes cream of tartar when purified.

Ark
Wooden or metal box, chest or bin, with a domed lid, for flour, fruit, corn, etc., suspended from the middle of the roof away from vermin.

Arming
A term applied to anything armoured, or that is part of a soldier's equipment, e.g. arming coat, arming sword.

Armory
1. *Aumbry.
2. The harness, saddle, and weapons for a horseman.

Arquebus
Portable gun, longer and larger than a musket, with a rest fastened to the barrel in order to support its weight when being fired.

Arras
A rich tapestry, in which figures and scenes are woven in colour; a hanging screen of this material. Originally from the town in Artois, France.

Arrearages
Arrears; payments overdue; debts.

Arrish Rake
Rake for the stubble.

Arrow Timber
Wood for making arrows.

Artificer
Craftsman.

Asafoetida
Resinous gum used as a flavouring in cookery, or medicinally.

Ash Balls
Wood ash bound together with oil, which could be used as soap because of its potassium content.

Ash Baukes

Beams made from ash trees.

Ashcloth
A cloth placed over the washtub with marshmallow leaves; water was poured through it to soften it before washing clothes. (Ssx)

Ash Kettle
Kettle containing wood ash, the main constituent of *lye used for washing clothes.

Ashen
A pail made of ash for carrying milk.

Assign
Person to whom a property is legally transferred, or who is delegated to act for another.

Auger
1. Carpenter's tool for boring holes in wood. It has a screw point and a handle at the top of the shaft by which it is screwed into the wood.
2. Metal bit attached to a carpenter's brace.

Aumbry
Wooden cupboard for keeping victuals (usually prepared food rather than stores), with openings for air to circulate, perhaps using *hair cloth as sides to allow circulation. May also be used to store clothes, linen, etc. or, in a church, books, vestments, vessels, etc.

Awl
Tool for piercing small holes in wood.

Axle Tree
The fixed wooden beam on the ends of which the wheels of a cart or waggon, etc. revolve; an axle.

Ayes
A harrow. (Gls)

Back
1. *Back Iron.
2. Chair back.

Back Band
Broad leather strap or iron chain, passing over a cart saddle and supporting the shafts of a vehicle.

Back Board
1. Board at the back of furniture, such as benches, chairs, stools and mirrors.
2. A wooden screen to exclude draughts.

3. A scored wooden board for making oat-cakes or rolling dough. (Ntt; Yks)

Back Board Chair
Chair with a solid back which could be converted into a table.

Back Crook
Iron hook hanging in the back of the hearth.

Back End
Out house; perhaps a bakery. (Lin; Yks)

Back House
1. Out-house or lean-to used as a kitchen, scullery, wash-house, etc.
2. *Bakehouse.

Back Hud, Plate
Iron fire back, usually with raised ornamentation. (Dby)

Back Iron
1. Fire-back, often ornamental, placed against the masonry of the chimney.
2. *Back stone.

Back Pan
Baking Pan.

Back Piece
*Back Iron.

Backsettle, Backside
The rear part of a property; the back yard or farm yard, perhaps with out-buildings.

Back, Baking Spittle
Flat wooden shovel or board used to place cakes, especially oat-cakes, in the oven. (Yks, Lan)

Back Stone
Flat plate of iron or stone (especially slate) on which oatcakes etc., were baked in an oven. It usually had a handle over the top.

Back Stool
Hard chair with a back but no arms.

Back Sword
Sword with only one cutting edge.

Backing Stock, Backitt
Fire back.

Bacon Frame
Rack for curing bacon, or hanging cured bacon, in the house. (Sts)

Bag
A dry measure of quantity or weight, varying by locality, and by the nature of the goods concerned.

Bagging Bill
*Bill for reaping peas, beans, corn, etc.

Bail, Bale
Hoop-handle of a kettle or similar vessel.

Bailiwick
Area of a bailiff's jurisdiction.

Baize, Bays
Originally a fine, light material introduced into England by Huguenot refugees in the 16th c; subsequently a coarse woollen cloth with a raised nap, made with a worsted warp and woollen weft, and used for curtains, coverings, etc.

Bake House
1. Building or room with an oven for baking.
2. Building or room at the back.

Baker Weight
Measure used for assessing the quantity of flour milled from a given quantity of grain.

Balance
1. *Valance.
2. Scales, often described as `a pair of', comprising a horizontal beam on a central pivot, with a pan at each end.

Balance Clock
Clock controlled by a rotating balance wheel.

Bald
1. Piebald; animal having a white streak on the face.
2. Barren.

Bales, Balls, Ballowes
Bellows.

Balet
Small bale.

Balk, Baulk
1. *Beam of a balance.
2. Roughly squared beam of wood.
3. A ridge, heap, or mound of earth, usually marking the end of a strip in the open fields, and originally formed by turning the plough,
4. A small cupboard in the ceiling close to the fire, for drying and storing meat; roof timbers from which meat was hung. (Dby, Yks)

Ballons
*Valance.

Ballrybb
A joint of pork cut from nearer the rump than the spare rib. (Bdf)

Ballys
Small rod. (Gls)

Balm Water
Medicinal preparation made from herbs.

Band
1. *Wearing band.
2. *Swaddle bands
2. Metal hoop on a wheel rim.
3. *Bond.
4. Hinges with long flat bands of iron fixed to the back of a door.
5. Pair of strips of thin white material worn by men, around the neck, with the ends hanging down in front.

Band String
Tasselled tie for fastening *bands.

Bandoleer
A leather shoulder belt to support a musket and carry cases containing cartridges or charges.

Bandore
A stringed musical instrument, resembling a guitar or lute and originating in Italy (where it was called a `pandora'). It was used as a bass to accompany a *cithern.

Bangle
Large rough stick, the cut branch of a tree. (War)

Bank
Bench or long seat.

Banker
1. Cloth used to cover a seat or bench; a cushion for a form. Various fabrics might be used.
2. An ornamental hanging or tapestry for a bed or a wall.
2. A long wooden work-bench, used in bricklaying or by masons.

Banking Iron
Long spade for digging ditches.

Banyan
Informal indoor gentleman's gown made of Indian cottons.

Bar
1. Bar of iron at the base of the chimney, from which pots could be suspended.

2. *Warping bar.

Bare
Used of a wain or cart without sides or covering, as opposed to *bound. (Dby, Ntt)

Bare Leap
Large open basket, carried by two men, for removing chaff from a barn. (Dby)

Barefoot Wheel, Bare Welys
Wheel without an iron rim

Bargain
A small farm holding.

Bark
1. A small ship.
2. Candle box, formerly made of bark.
3. Bark used in tanning and dyeing.

Bark Bing
Tool for beating bark in tanning.

Barker
One who works with bark in the tanning and dyeing industry.

Barkham, Barquam
Pad on a horse's collar taking the pressure of the wooden or metal harness; a flat piece of leather protecting the horse's neck from rain. (Dby, Yks)

Bark House
Tanning house; place where bark is stored.

Bark Tub
Tub for storing bark, used in tanning.

Barking Iron
Tool used for stripping bark from trees.

Barleape
A large basket.

Barley Mow
Rick or stack of barley.

Barley Roll
1. Wooden cylinder pressed down and rolled across a heap of barley to separate the grain from the awns. (Gls)
2. A cart. (Bkm)

Barlines
*Traces. (Ess)

Barm
The foamy yeast which forms on fermenting *malt liquor, used to leaven bread.

Barm Skin
A leather apron.

Barm Tub

Tub used for fermentation in brewing.

Barnacle

A device inserted into a horse's nose by the blacksmith to keep it quiet whilst being shod.

Barnstaple Oven

Ovens manufactured from local grit in the Barnstaple area; once heated by wood or furze fires, the grit retained sufficient heat to bake the bread or meat placed inside it when the ashes were removed.

Barras

Coarse linen fabric originally imported from the Low Countries.

Barrateen

A woven fabric.

Barred Chest

Chest used for travelling, reinforced and protected by iron bands and bars.

Barrel

Vessel smaller than a *hogshead in which liquids could be stored.

Barrey

Hand barrow. (Dur)

Barrow Hog, Pig

Castrated boar.

Barton

Farmyard, or enclosed area of ground used for a specific agricultural purpose, e.g. a rick barton.

Bartree

Wooden frame for the warp.

Base Court

Court or yard at the back of a house, or perhaps in a castle or mansion, with its out-buildings; often occupied by servants.

Base(s)

1. Trestles.

2. Plaited skirt of cloth, velvet, or rich brocade, appended to a *doublet, and reaching from the waist to the knees.

3. The hangings of a bed, especially those which hang to the floor at the sides and feet.

Baselard

Long dagger or short sword, usually worn at the *girdle, with a hilt shaped like a capital H on its side.

Basils, Bassell Skins

Sheepskins tanned in *bark, used especially in book-binding.

Basin

Used for washing hands during the meal (forks were not used).

Bason

1. Bench with a plate of iron, or a stone flag set in it, and a fire underneath, on which the first part of the felting process in hatting was performed.

2. *Basin.

Bass, Bast

Fibrous material from the phloem of certain plants such as flax, hemp, rushes, etc., used to make matting or rope; the matting itself.

Bass Chair

Rush-seated chair, often with sides and back made of straw coils in a wooden frame.

Bastard

Of poor quality.

Bastet

Sack or rough plaited basket to contain wool. (Nfk)

Basting Ladle

A ladle used to baste mead, that is, pour fat, cooking juices, or other liquid over roasting mead to prevent it drying out whilst cooking.

Bath Stove

A hot grate with an iron plate above the fire.

Battery

Metalwork wrought by hammering.

Battledore

1. Leaf of paper mounted on a tablet of wood, with a handle and protective translucent horn, containing the alphabet, and perhaps also numerals, the Lord's Prayer, and other basic reading matter.

2. Wooden utensil used for mangling or smoothing clothes after washing.

Baulkes and Skales

Beam and balance for weighing.

Bavin

A bundle of brushwood, bound with one band or *withy branch only, rather than two, as in the case of a *faggot.

Bawdekin

Rich brocade; originally woven with

woof of silk and warp of gold.

Bawtree Measure
A measure of lead, the market for which was at Bawtree. (Dby)

Bay
1. A reddish brown colour, generally used of horses.
2. The division of a house or barn.
3. *Baize.

Bay Oil
An oil obtained from the berries of laurel or bay trees, in appearance like butter.

Bay Salt
Coarse salt obtained by evaporating sea-water under the sun's heat.

Bayard
A hand barrow used for heavy loads, often associated with fireside equipment. (Bdf)

Beads
String of beads to keep count of prayers, often in `pairs'; a rosary.

Beak, Beck
Pointed end of an anvil.

Beaker
A large drinking vessel with a wide mouth.

Beam
1. *Beam and weights.
2. The wooden cylinder or roller in a loom on which the warp is wound before weaving, or the roller onto which the cloth is wound as it is woven.
3. The principal timber of a plough, to which everything else is fixed.
4. A crescent shaped piece of iron, raised at one end, on which raw hides were scraped with a *beam knife.

Beam and Weights
A pair of scales with the weights. The beam, strictly speaking, was the transverse bar of the scales, but the term was often applied to the whole scales.

Beam Knife
A long, heavy, curved knife used by tanners to remove hair from skins.

Bear
Case, as in *pillow bere.

Bearing
Term applied to items that are suitable for carrying, e.g. baskets, buckets, tubs, etc.

Bearing Cloth, Mantle, Sheet
A baby's christening robe, or cloth used in child-bearing.

Beat
Turf pared off for burning.

Beating Block
Block used by craftsmen such as coopers and glaziers for beating things into shape.

Beating Horse
Frame for beating clothes on.

Beattell
A wooden club or hammer used for driving wedges or pegs. (Bdf)

Beattrihers
A beating axe, i.e. an implement used to break up sods for burning. (Con)

Beaupers
Fabric used for flags.

Beaver Hat
Superior felt hat made from beaver fur.

Beckhorn
Anvil with points at both ends.

Bed
1. The mattress only, which might be stuffed with *flock, feathers, down, etc.
2. The body of a cart.

Bed Boards
The wooden planks which form the base of the bed, laid across the *bed stock.

Bed Case
Wooden bedstead, or a mattress cover. (Gls)

Bed Cord
Cord threaded through a bed frame to provide support for the *bed.

Bed Couch
Day bed. (Lin)

Bed Hilling
*Hilling.

Bed Mat
A mat laid on the bed cords underneath a *bed.

Bed Performed
Bed fully set up, complete with mattress, etc.

Bed Staves
*Bed boards.

Bed Stock

The front and back of a bed, especially its posts, between which the *bed boards were laid. Sometimes referred to as a `pair'.

Bed Tick, Tye
*Tick.

Beddered Woman
Bedmaker, i.e. an upholsterer.

Bederoll
List of those remembered in *obits - often benefactors of the church.

Bedesman
One who prays for the soul or spiritual welfare of another.

Bedstead
The wooden framework of a bed.

Bee
A ring or torque. (Con)

Bee Cote, Skep, Stall
Hive.

Beef in Powder
Salted beef.

Beef Pyke
*Flesh crook.

Beer
*Pillow bere

Beer Stool
Stand for a cask of beer. (Nfk; Sfk)

Beeregar
Sour vinegar made from beer.

Beetle
Heavy headed wooden hammer or mallet used to hammer stakes into the ground, ram wedges, beat or crush flax and hemp, etc., and having various shapes, dependant on the task for which it was used.

Beetle Ring
Iron ring used to strengthen the heads of a *beetle.

Beeyn
Bee hive. (War)

Belchild
Grandchild (Sfk)

Belfry
Temporary shed or rick-stand made of materials such as straw, furze, sticks, or wood, used as a shelter for animals, agricultural implements, beasts, etc. (Lin)

Bell Glass
A bell-shaped glass frame or cloche,

used for forcing plant-growth in the spring.

Bell Metal
An alloy of copper and tin, or sometimes zinc and lead, used for casting bells and some domestic wares.

Bellises, Billowe
Bellows.

Bellow Boards
Wooden sides of a bellows.

Belly Band
Band which passes around the body of a horse to check the play of the shafts.

Belting Hurdle
Hurdle used to shelter animals. (War)

Bench, Bench Board
Long form with a wooden backrest; the frame of the bench may be mentioned separately from the `board', i.e. the seat. Sometimes fixed to the wall.

Bench Cloth
Cushion or cloth for a *bench.

Bend
The belting for the wheels of mill machinery. (Sts)

Bend Leather
Thick leather used for soles of boots and shoes; the stoutest type of leather.

Bend of Leather
Half an oxhide, with the thinner parts cut off.

Bender
A mechanical device for setting or drawing cross-bows.

Bene
Bees. (Chs)

Benjamin
An aromatic gum used for perfuming gloves.

Bents
Rushes or reeds.

Bereloy
A carrying basket. (Nth)

Besom
A brush made from twigs of broom, heather, birch, etc., tied together around a handle; a broom.

Bibb
Small tankard. (Gls)

Bice
A dull azure colour.

Bickern, Bickhorn

Small anvil, with two tapering ends.

Bidet
Vessel on a low narrow stand, which can be bestriden when taking a bath.

Bigg
Poor quality barley, coarse but hardy, which grows quickly on poor soils; used for malting.

Biggen
Child's cap; nightcap. (Dor; Ham)

Biliment, Biliment Lace
Ornament worn by a woman on her head or neck; ornamental lace.

Bill
1. An infantry weapon of various forms, ranging from a concave blade on a long handle, to an axe with a spike on its back and the shaft ending in a spearhead; a *halberd.
2. A tool used in hedging, copse clearing, etc; a crescent-shaped blade often with a sharp hook. Its form varied greatly from place to place, and depended also on its specific purpose.
3. A chisel for cutting grooves in mill-stones. (Ess)
4. *Bill Obligatory.

Bill Obligatory
A written statement acknowledging a debt and promising to pay it at a specified date.

Billet
1. Thick firewood.
2. Stick used as a weapon.
3. Small bar of metal.

Binding
Braid, banding or fastening; cloth that secures the raw edges of a piece of fabric.

Binding Money
Premium paid to the master of an apprentice.

Binding Thread
Twine used to bind sheaves of corn.

Bing
1. *Bark bing.
2. A bin or box for corn or flour.
3. A manger. (Sal)

Bing Stone
The stone on which bark was beaten. (Dby)

Binge

Instrument for beating bark for the tanning industry. (Chs)

Bink
Wooden shelf or frame of shelves for storing earthenware or pewter; a plate rack or dresser. (Northern)

Bird Bolt
A short, thick arrow, with a flat end, used to kill birds without piercing them.

Bird Broach, Spit
Small spit for cooking poultry or game birds.

Bird Work
Embroidery depicting birds.

Birding Piece
*Fowling piece or shot-gun.

Birds Eye
Rectangular ornamentation on fabric.

Bit Bridle
Mouth-piece of a bridle.

Black Cup
Leather drinking vessel, coated with tar or pitch. (Dby)

Black Jack
1. Large leather beer jug, coated with tar.
2. Zinc sulphide; a mining term.

Black Work
1. Type of embroidery done in black silk on linen.
2. In mining, any dark-coloured stratum.

Blackloge
Black lamb fur. (Nth)

Blacks
Mourning clothes.

Blackthorn
Primus spinoza, used for making cutlery handles.

Blades
Shafts of a cart or wain.

Blank Table
A plain, scrubbed, kitchen table.

Blend Corn
Mixture of wheat and rye sown together.

Blinds
Blinkers on a horse harness.

Block
1. Piece of wood used in fastening a heel to a shoe.

2. Square cut timber.

3. A large piece of wood used as a work surface for chopping, hammering, etc.

Blocks
Sections of a mould used for shaping hats. The mould consisted of several variously shaped blocks which could be put together to form different shapes.

Blood Iron
*Fleam.

Blowing House
Tin smelting house (Con)

Bluet
A bluish woollen cloth.

Blunderbuss
Flintlock gun with a wide bore, capable of firing many pellets; for short-range use.

Boar Frank
Enclosure for boars; pigsty.

Board
Timber plank forming the top of a table. Trestles are itemised separately. May also be a plank for other purposes, depending on the context, e.g. for a market stall.

Board Carpet
*Board cloth.

Board Chair
Chair for sitting at table.

Board Chest
Chest made from boards pegged or pinned together, rather than jointed.

Board Cloth
Table cloth.

Board Shave
Carpenter's plane.

Board with a Frame
*Framed Table.

Boarded
Made of boards nailed or pinned together, rather than jointed.

Boarded Bedstead
*Bedstead with panelled or *wainscot head-board and/or foot.

Bob Wig
Wig with curls turned up into `bobs' at the bottom.

Bobbin Lace
Lace made on a pillow with bobbins.

Bodge
Measure of oats; half a peck.

Bodice
Linen garment for the upper part of a woman's body, strengthened with whalebone; also that part of a woman's dress above the waist, made separately from the *kirtle but attached to it.

Bodkin
1. A bar forming part of the tackle for a plough or harrow. (Dor)

2. Long hair-pin used by women. (Lan)

3. Small pointed instrument of bone, iron or steel for making holes in cloth.

Body Girt
Belly band of a saddle; *Girse.

Boes
1. A plasterer's tray or hod. (Chs)

2. A hassock or seat made of straw.

Boiling Iron
*Brandreth.

Bole Armeniac
Pale, reddish earth from Armenia, used medicinally, and also as a constituent in gold size and canvas priming.

Bolling Lace
Bobbled lace. (Dur)

Bolster
1. A long stuffed pillow on which the head is rested whilst in bed.

2. The block or plate on which metal to be punched is laid.

3. The solid lump of steel or other material between the tang and the blade of a wheelwrights knife.

Bolt
1. A bundle of reeds or straw, of a specific weight or size.

2. A roll of woven fabric, generally of a definite length.

3. An arrow for use with a cross-bow; generally short and stout.

4. A flour sieve, a sifter.

Bolting
Sifting or sieving corn: the process of separating the flour from the husk.

Bolting Cloth
Fine cloth used for *bolting.

Bolting House
Room where flour is sifted and bread made.

Bolting Hutch, Mill, Tub, Tun, Which

Tub or bin into which grain is sifted from the husks, or flour from the bran.

Bombasine
Twilled or corded worsted material; cotton or silk was sometimes added. In black, the material was much used for mourning clothes.

Bond
Promissory note or deed under which money was lent, or administrators and executors were required to perform their legal functions. It included a penalty for failure to comply with its conditions.

Bone Lace
Made from linen thread, with bone bobbins.

Book Debt
Money owed to a craftsman or other trader, and recorded in his account book.

Boose, Bowse
Cattle stall. (Lin; Yks)

Boose Stake
Wooden post where cows were tied in the cow house. (Dby)

Boot Hose
Men's over-stockings, worn inside boots to prevent the under-hose becoming soiled by the boot leather.

Boot Jack
Contrivance for pulling boots off.

Boot Tree
A foot-shaped piece of wood inserted into a boot or shoe to keep it in shape.

Borax
A type of salt used in dyeing.

Borrenger
*Porringer

Borwte Hammer
*Boute.

Boskin
Wooden partition in a cow-house, with a ring for tying up cattle. (Dby)

Boss
1. A plasterers hod or tray.
2. A seat of straw.

Botham
Skein or ball of thread or yarn. (Sts)

Bothies
1. A store house or shop. (Dby)
2. A water course. (Dby)

Bottams
Balls of yarn. (Bdf)

Bottle
1. A small container for carrying liquor, probably made of leather.
2. A round moulding. (Oxf)
3. A bundle, especially firewood or hay.

Bouch, Bouk, Bowk
Bucket; wooden pail with an upright handle.

Boule
Type of handle. (Lin)

Boulter
A long fishing line with many hooks. Open-weave fabric used in a sieve.

Bound
Used of a *wain or cart with sides, and perhaps a covering, as opposed to *bare. (Northern)

Bound Wheel
Wheel with iron rim.

Boure
Bower: a chamber.

Boute
Blacksmith's heavy, two-handed hammer.

Bow
1. *Ox Bow.
2. *Bow Hurdle.
3. The semi-circular handle of a pail.
4. A stall for cattle. (War)
5. A high fire-guard. (Oxf)
6. Part of a *tumbrel. (War)
7. Weapon: usually a long-bow.

Bow Chair
Chair with a bow-shaped back.

Bow Dye
Scarlet dye from the dye-house at Bow, in East London.

Bow Hurdle
A six-foot pole with projecting ends, over which a string of catgut (a `bow') was drawn; the material from which hats were made was stretched on this. (Gls; Oxf)

Bow Saw
Saw with a narrow blade set in a strong frame.

Bow Stave
The wooden part of a bow for shooting arrows.

Bow String
String for an archery bow, or for a
hatter's bow.

Bowbarde
*Cupboard. (Ham)

Bowlstering
Perverting or abusing the law.

Box
Wood of the box tree.

Box Iron
A hollow, triangular-shaped iron, in
which hot coals could be placed, for
smoothing clothes.

Boxes
Small lided chest without feet,
intended to rest on a table. (Bdf)

Brach Pan
*Dripping Pan. (Gls)

Bracken Ashes
Ash from bracken was rolled into balls
and used to make *lye (in place of
soap).

Braid, Bread
Board for pressing curd in cheese-
making. (Sfk)

Brake
1. *Bread Brake.
2. A toothed instrument for breaking
flax or hemp.
3. A heavy *harrow for breaking clods
in rough ground.
4. A snaffle or bridle for a horse.
5. A framework intended to hold
something steady, e.g. a horse's foot
when being shod, a strainer placed
over a tub.
6. A cart without a body, used in
breaking horses. (Oxf)
7. A large barrow. (Oxf)
8. A hook or sickle for up-rooting
grass. (Gls)
9. A wooden mill for crushing green
fruit and hops. (Bdf)
10. A cage or trap. (Bdf)

Brake Board
*Bread Brake (2).

Brake Stool
Stand on which hemp was placed to be
crushed.

Branched Stuff, Branchis
Textiles or fabrics with raised patterns.

Branches, Branch Candle
Chandeliers, often made of brass, with
a number of arms or branches.

Brand Iron
1. Branding iron, used for burning
marks of ownership in livestock.
2. *Brandred.

Branded Heifer
Heifer with burnt-on mark of
ownership.

Branded Wheat
Wheat affected by a fungoid disease,
which makes it appear burnt.

Brandlett
1. *Brand Iron.
2. Stand for a cask or hay-rick. (Bdf)
3. Iron framework on which to rest
kitchen utensils. (Bdf)

Brandred, Brandreth, Brandize
1. *Gridiron or *trivet used to support
cooking vessels over an open fire.
2. A wooden framework to support,
e.g., barrels, hay stacks, etc.
3. A rail or fence surrounding a well.

Brank
Buckwheat.

Brasen, Brason
Made of brass. Brass pots were
stronger than *latten; they were also
better than iron, as they could be
repaired.

Brass Faces
Ornamentation on *andirons.

Brass Pieces
Counters for a *shuffleboard.

Brawn
A fattened boar.

Bray
1. Tool used in breaking hemp.
2. Horse bit.
3. Small piece of charcoal used in
refining iron. (Wor)

Braying Stone
Used like a pestle for pounding in a
mortar.

Brazil
1. Scarlet dye from a redwood tree of
the East Indies, and also of a South
American species (from which the
country is named); also, material dyed
with it.
2. Brazil nut.

Brazil Pepper

Brazil nut.

Breach Field
A field newly ploughed from fallow, ready for sowing.

Bread Brake, Fleake
1. Slatted wooden box or hurdle suspended from the ceiling for storing bread.
2. A kneading trough.

Bread Grate
*Bread brake.

Break Horn
*Bickern.

Breast Plate
Harness strap running across a horse's breast.

Breast Whimble
A king of auger or gimlet upon which the breast presses in working.

Brede
Piece of material of the full width. (Dur)

Breeches
Short trousers fastened beneath the knee, covering the loins and thigh.

Breeder
Animal capable of breeding; often in-calf cows.

Brentis
Black or dark colour. (Nth)

Breviary
Book containing the daily offices, for use of clergy.

Brew House
Room or out-house set aside for brewing.

Brewing Gutts
A pipe or sink for liquid to flow out.

Brewing Keive
*Keive

Bribe
Piece cut off an end of cloth, which is damaged or imperfect; a short length of cloth. (Yks)

Bridges Satin
*Bruges.

Bridgwater
Woollen cloth originally from Bridgwater, Somerset.

Brigandine
Body armour consisting of iron rings or small plates, sewed on canvas, linen or leather, and covered by similar material; originally in two halves, hence a `pair of ...'. Worn by foot soldiers.

Brigg
1. Iron frame, often hinged, supporting pots and pans over the hearth. (Yks)
2. Wooden frame to support a *sile when draining curds in cheese-making, or the *temps when separating the *malt from the *wort in brewing.

Briggs
*Brogues

Brimstone
Sulphur, used medicinally.

Brindle, Brinded
Tawny brown, marked with streaks of a different hue.

Bristol Shot
Lead shot made in Bristol.

Broach
1. Spit for roasting.
2. A chisel.
3. A piercing instrument.

Broad Cloth, Broads
Fine, plain, black, hard-wearing cloth, weaved two yards wide with a short nap, used for men's outer clothing.

Broad Gold, Piece
Gold coins struck by hammer, superseded after 1663 by the guinea, although legal tender until 1733; worth 20s. They were much broader and thinner than the new coinage.

Broad Loom
Loom (2) for weaving *Broad cloth.

Broad Silk
A wide piece of silk, as opposed to a ribbon.

Broad Weaver
Weaver of *broadcloth.

Brocatelle
Fabric similar to brocade, of silk or wool, used for tapestry, upholstery, etc.

Brod
Round-headed nail made by a blacksmith.

Brogues
Leather breeches.

Broiling Iron, Plate
1. A support for a cooking pot; a *grid

iron.

2. A type of Dutch oven.

Brok

Bracket: a small shelf, usually ornamental, for the wall of a room.

Brome

Variety of grass resembling oats.

Broom Hook

Hook for clearing undergrowth, especially broom or gorse.

Brown Holland

Unbleached *Holland cloth.

Browse

Brushwood, furze, etc., for kindling fires.

Brush Hook

*Bill for cutting brushwood.

Bruges

A type of satin made in Bruges, Flanders.

Brushing Chamber

Room for dressing or smoothing flax.

Brussels Carpet

Carpet with a worsted warp brought to the surface in loops to make the pile. Originally made in Brussels.

Buck

1. Body of a cart or waggon, especially its front.

2. Buckwheat: coarse wheat for animal feed.

Buck Iron

Grooved iron used for making horse-shoes. (Gls)

Bucking

The process of steeping clothes in *lye to cleanse them, when soap was rare and expensive. After steeping, the clothes were beaten with flat wooden bats; also applied to the clothes themselves.

Bucking Basket

Washing or clothes basket.

Bucking Cooler, Loom, Tub

Tub used in the process of *bucking.

Buckler

Small round shield for personal defence, strapped to the left arm, or carried by a handle at the back.

Buckling Chains

Chains for the harness of horse or oxen.

Buckram

Fine linen or cotton; subsequently coarse linen stiffened with paste or gum.

Bud

Bull, bullock or heifer aged one to two years.

Budge

Lambskin, with the wool dressed outside to resemble fur.

Budget

1. Milk can shaped to be carried on the back.

2. A workman's bag, pouch, or wallet, usually of leather, and perhaps carried on horse-back.

Budget Kettle

Small portable flask or billy-can.

Buff Coat

Soldier's coat of stout leather dressed with oil, which provided some protection against weapons such as swords.

Buffet

An early form of sideboard, with three shelves, some or all of which were open to display pewter etc.

Buffet Stool

Low stool with an upholstered seat, set on a frame for use at table; a footstool.

Buffin

Coarse cloth used for gowns; a garment made of this material.

Bugle

Tube-shaped glass bead, usually black, worn as jewellery.

Bulchin

Bull calf.

Bulk

Framework projecting from the front of a shop or stall.

Bullaines, Bullions

1. Bullion.

2. Gold or silver lace or braid.

3. Hooks or studs for fastening garments.

Bullen

Brass weights. (Oxf)

Bullymonge

A mixture of grains, such as oats, peas, and vetches, grown together; *maslin. (Bdf)

Bumble
Woven bull rushes, used for seating, etc.

Bunching Block
Wooden block on which hemp or flax was beaten with a *beetle. (Nfk; Sfk)

Buntin
Fir cone (Dur)

Bunting
A piece of squared timber.

Bunting Trough
Trough used in the process of bunting, i.e., sieving bran from the wheaten flour after it has been ground.

Burden
A measure of hay or straw; as much as can be carried by a man, or by a cart.

Burdit
Cotton fabric.

Burgage
A freehold property in a borough, a house held by burgage tenure.

Burgundy Pitch
The resinous juice of the spruce fir, from Neufchatel (formerly in Burgundy).

Burling
1. Yearling bullock or heifer.
2. The process of rectifying faults in newly made cloth.

Burling Iron
Clothier's iron for removing unevenness in cloth.

Burn
Branding iron. (Dby)

Burnet
Brown woollen cloth of fine quality.

Burnt China
China that is painted after the initial decorations, and re-fired.

Burnt Silver
Silver calcined for use as a drug or pigment.

Burrier
Tool for picking and *burling woollen cloth. (Dev)

Burthen
A load; the carrying capacity of a ship.

Bushel
1. A dry measure of capacity used for corn, etc., varying in quantity according to locality, but generally equal to four pecks or eight gallons; a vessel holding this amount.
2. The iron rim of a wheel, which prevents it from wearing. (Dur)

Busk
A strip of wood or whale-bone used in a woman's stays or corsets to stiffen and support them.

Buskin
A light leather or cloth covering for the feet and lower legs; a half-boot or leather gaiters.

Buss
1. A young calf.
2. Wooden frame at the top of a wall. (Oxf)

Bustian
A cotton fabric used for waistcoats, sometimes described as a coarse type of *fustian, sometimes distinct from it.

Bustimes
A cotton fabric. (Con)

Butt
1. A cask for wine or ale, its capacity varying between 108 and 140 gallons.
2. The thicker part of anything, especially hides and skins, or the end of anything.
3. A heavy two-wheeled cart, made to tip. (Dev)
4. A small piece of land in an open field, usually of irregular shape.
5. Basket for catching fish, especially salmon.
6. A bee-hive.

Butter
1. Small tub for washing butter.
2. *Bolting cloth.
3. Blacksmith's tool.

Butterkits
Square boxes for carrying butter to market on horseback. (Dur)

Buttery
Store room for drink and food; a cool room as opposed to the kitchen.

Butt Maund
Basket fitted with two lids used for carrying butter and eggs.

Buttress
Tool used to pare horses' hooves before shoeing.

Byland

Headland in an open field, usually
unploughed, and perhaps used as a
footpath between the strips. (Chs)

Byrne Hooks
Large hooks suspended from pack
saddles, for carrying additional
burdens. (Dby)

Cab
A dry measure of capacity.

Cabinet
Originally a box for valuables, but,
by 1700, it had become a substantial
piece of furniture, with compartments,
drawers and shelves concealed by
doors which opened outwards.

Cabriole
Leg of a table or other piece of
furniture, curved outwards at the knee,
and tapering inwards below, with an
ornamental foot.

Cad
The youngest and smallest animal;
especially used of pigs.

Cadawe, Caddow
A coarse woollen covering, made in
Ireland, and used as a horse blanket or
a bed covering.

Caddis
1. Material such as wool, cotton, etc.,
used to pad clothes.
2. A worsted tape used for garters and
*girdles.
3. A coarse, cheap serge.

Cade
1. Young animal abandoned by its
mother and fed by hand.
2. A barrel of herrings.

Cade Coals
Coal for domestic use. (War)

Cader
Cradle, scaffolding.

Cades
Shreds of any material. (Wor)

Cadow
A rough woollen bed covering. (Chs)

Caffa
Rich silk cloth similar to *damask.

Cage
Open fronted cupboard for glassware
etc.

Cake Print
Baker's implement for making small
cakes. (Dby; Sts)

Cake Sprittle
Thin board for turning oat-cakes
during cooking.

Calaber
Fur from a foreign species of squirrel,
perhaps originally imported from
Calabria.

Calamanco
A fine woollen satin-twilled stuff,
checked or brocaded, and glossy on
the surface, made in Flanders. Much
used for waistcoats and *breeches in
the 18th c.

Calash
A light carriage with removable folding
hood and low wheels.

Calbot
*Cobiron. (Sal)

Caldern
*Cauldron

Calfreting Board
Plank suitable for caulking. (Con)

Calico
A general name for light cotton cloths,
originally plain, but later frequently
printed with designs, and glazed,
originally imported from Calicut,
India, but subsequently made in
England.

Calimanco
A glazed woollen cloth from Flanders,
with a glazed surface and a chequered
or diamond pattern, used for
*petticoats.

Caliver
1. A light musket or blunderbuss; the
lightest fire-arm available apart from
the *pistol, fired without a rest. It
could fire ball shot or short arrows.
2. A draught horse collar. (Dur)

Caliver Flask
Leather or metal case holding
gunpowder.

Calkins
The parts of a horse-shoe which are
turned down and sharpened to prevent
slipping.

Call
1. Dish shelf or rack. (Yks)
2. Close fitting cap for women.

3. Whistle.

Call of Gold
Ornamental net-work.

Callis Sand
A fine white sand, originally from Calais, used for blotting ink, and for scouring and cleaning pewter.

Camber
Chamber.

Cambrel
Butcher's hook for hanging carcasses.

Cambric, Camerick
A type of fine white linen, originally made at Cambrai, in France. The term was also applied to a hand-spun cotton imitation.

Came
Grooved bars of lead which held the glass in lattice windows.

Camlet
A fine, light linen made from combination of wool, silk and hair, and especially from the wool of angora goats. It is said to have originally been made from camel hair in the Middle East, but this is uncertain. Frequently used for bed hangings, upholstery, and women's clothing.

Camp Chair
Folding chair.

Campernows
Ale potage made with sugar and spice.

Can
1. A cylindrical vessel for holding liquid; a drinking vessel, not necessarily metal.
2. A bucket for milk or water.

Cancase
A box of pins or combs used in wool-combing.

Canch
A small rick, adjoining another. (Bdf)

Candle Case
Case or box for candles.

Candle Branch
1. Socket to place a candle.
2. Chandelier.

Candle Mould
Pewter or tin mould for making candles.

Candle Plate
Metal plate with a *pricket-type spike

to take a candle, or a single socket on a round plate.

Canhook
Short rope or chain with a flat hook at each end, used for slinging a cask (Dur)

Cannell
Bituminous, bright-burning coal that could be cut and polished like jet. Occasionally used for candlesticks and other small objects.

Cannequin
A white cotton cloth from the East Indies.

Canopy
*Hangings (2) suspended over a bed.

Canstick
Candlestick, originally using a *pricket rather than a socket to hold the candle.

Cantch
Small amount of unthreshed corn. (War)

Cantle
Fragment or remnant.

Canterbury
Stand to hold music portfolios.

Cantharides
Dried beetle, used for medicinal purposes.

Cantoon
A strong *fustian, with fine cording on one side, and a smooth bright finish on the other.

Canvas
Coarse, unbleached cloth made from hemp or flax, used especially for window curtains and for supporting mattresses, and very popular for *doublets.

Cap Case
1. Travelling bag or wallet for personal belongings.
2. Box, chest or casket; a receptacle of any kind.

Cap Cloak
Cloak with a hood.

Cap Paper
1. Wrapping paper.
2. A size of writing paper.

Cap Staff
Capstan or crane.

Capers
Flower buds of the caper (a shrub), gathered for pickling.

Caple, Capul
Horse. (Northern)

Caplin
The strong leather loop or hinge on a flail.

Capon
Castrated cock being fattened for the table.

Caponet
A small or young *capon.

Capouche
A hood or cowl, especially that of Capuchin monks.

Car
Four-wheeled vehicle. (War)

Car Slide
A type of sledge.

Carbine
A short, light musket, accurate in fire, but with a short range; used by cavalry.

Carchew, Carchowe, Carcheife
*Kerchief

Card
Iron toothed comb set in leather, used to part and comb out fibres of wool or flax in preparation for spinning, or to raise the nap on cloth. Used in pairs, one of which was a fixed *stock card, the other held in the hand.

Card Leaves
The sheets of leather into which the teeth of *cards were inserted.

Card Table, Pair of
Table used for playing cards, consisting of two boards hinged together which, when opened, formed a table. Often covered in cloth or *baize.

Cardinals Hat
A flat, broad-rimmed dish. (Ham)

Carding Stock
*Stock card.

Care Sunday
The fifth Sunday in Lent, or the Sunday immediately preceding Good Friday; also referred to as Passion Sunday.

Carl Hemp
The seed-bearing hemp plant, of stronger growth and coarser fibre than the male plant. `Carl' means male, but the name was mistakenly given to the female plant. Used in rope-making.

Carlin
A Neapolitan silver coin worth about four pence, or, later, two pence.

Carnacon
Rosy-pink coloured.

Carob
Fruit or pod of a Levantine tree.

Carpet
Heavily woven wool used as bed coverings or table cloths, etc. Not usually for the floor, except in the houses of the very wealthy.

Carpet Cushion
Thin cushion for benches and seating.

Carr
Marshy land, bog, or fen, perhaps with willows, alders, etc., growing on it.

Carral
A play pen for children. (Lin)

Carrel, Carrey
Mixed fabric of worsted and silk, or sometimes linen yarn.

Carriage
A wheeled vehicle generally; most likely to refer to a cart rather than anything grander in most probate records.

Carsey
*Kersey

Cart
A two-wheeled farm vehicle, smaller than a *wain, without springs.

Cart Bodies
That part of a cart which holds the load.

Cart Clout
Iron plate protecting the cart's axle from wear.

Cart Gear
Harness by which horses are attached to the cart.

Cart Saddle
Small saddle for a horse's back, to support the shafts.

Cart Staves
Poles, rods, etc., used on carts to hold the load on.

Cart Traces
Ropes, chains, or straps connecting a

horse's collar to the *swingletree.

Carthen
*Cauldron.

Carthamus
Bastard saffron, whose flowers yield red and yellow dyes.

Carvel Board
Plank of uniform thickness for building a ship in carvel style, i.e., laid side by side, not overlapping. (Con)

Case
1. Wooden container for a chamber pot.
2. Chest of drawers.
3. *Bed case. (Gls)
4. A hen hutch. (Bdf)

Casement
Frame forming a window, on hinges, attached to one of the uprights of the frame in which it is fixed.

Caser
A coarse sieve. (Dur)

Cask
A barrel of indeterminate size.

Cask Chair
Chair made from a cask or barrel.

Caslin
Inferior calf skin. (Sal)

Casselty
A *desperate debt.

Cassock
A long loose coat or gown, worn by both sexes.

Cast Back
Iron fire-back.

Caster
1. Best quality beaver fur; hats made of this, or of a rabbit skin imitation.
2. Small container with perforated top for sugar or pepper etc.

Caster Hat
Hat made of beaver fur, or, later, rabbit-skin.

Castile Soap
Fine, hard soap from Spain made with olive oil and soda.

Castilion
A type of cloth.

Casting Net
Fishing net that swept the bottom of the river.

Casting Shovel
Large shovel for casting grain in winnowing.

Castling
Calf born before the usual time.

Cather
*Cader

Cathern, Cawthern
*Cauldron.

Catshid
A sawn plank. (Gls)

Cattle
The word for goods, *`chattel', derived from the word `cattle'. The number of cattle was the measure of a man's wealth, and hence the word changed its meaning to `goods', as well as changing its pronunciation.

Caudle
A warm drink: thin gruel mixed with wine or ale, sweetened and spiced, mainly for the sick and their visitors.

Caudle Cup
Two-handled cup, perhaps with a lid, for drinking *posset or *caudle.

Caul Rope
Rope made from coarse hemp. (Oxf)

Cauldron
Large metal vessel with three legs for cooking, sometimes made of brass, standing over the fire, for stews, etc.

Caverings
Chaff or corn husks used to fill a mattress. (Sfk)

Caverwell Pott
A pot in which all of its contents are covered. (Dur)

Cawfoy
*Kersey.

Cawse
Causeway.

Ceever
*Kiver

Ceiled
*Sealed.

Ceiling
*Sellyng.

Cellar
A store-room for provisions; a granary, *buttery, or pantry, which could be above or below ground.

Cellar of Glasses
Box for holding drinks and glasses

Cellaret
Case or sideboard for storing wine bottles.

Cellot
*Skillet. (Gls)

Celour
1. A canopy over a bed, or its hangings.
2. Wall tapestry or screen of drapery.

Cerce
*Searce: a sieve or strainer.

Cereclothing
Placing a corpse in a *winding sheet.

Certum
A garland. (Lin)

Cess
1. Toilet.
2. Tax, rate or fee.

Cettle
1. *Settle.
2. *Kettle.

Chafer
A small, closed, transportable brazier containing burning charcoal or hot ash, on which a *chafing dish was placed.

Chaff Bed
Mattress filled with chaff and husks of corn.

Chafing Dish
A dish to put on a *chafer, to keep food warm.

Chain Lace
Braid lace, made from a single cord knotted upon itself.

Chain
1. A part of the harness attached to *butts, *ploughs, *trees and *yokes, etc.
2. Warp.

Chair Cart
A light cart, a *chaise, drawn by one horse.

Chair Chest
A wooden chair with arms, usually panelled, with a seat on hinges which lifted to reveal storage space.

Chair Stool
Chair with a back but no arms; stool with a back.

Chair Table
Chair with a solid back which could be folded down on to its arms to form a table.

Chaise
Light open carriage for travelling.

Chaise Mayrez
Cart for transporting fresh fish. (Gls)

Chalder
A dry measure, varying in quantity from 32 to 40 *bushels, for coal, lime, fish, etc.

Chaldron
1. *Cauldron.
2. *Chalder.

Chalk Line
Cord rubbed with chalk, used to lay down a straight line on material as a guide for cutting.

Chamber
Any room, excluding the hall or the kitchen, used for any purpose, but often an upstairs bedroom, and sometimes a parlour; a private room.

Cham(b)let
*Camlet.

Champion
Land in open fields divided into strips, as opposed to land held in *severalty.

Chandler
1. Candlestick; chandelier.
2. Candlestick maker or trader.
3. A dealer in groceries, provisions, etc.

Changeable
A fabric of changeable colour, either shot or variegated; often silk.

Chantry
Endowment for a priest to say mass for souls of specified dead; often refers to the chapel or altar where such masses were said.

Chape
1. Metal plate of a scabbard, especially that which covers the point; the scabbard itself.
2. One of the metal hooks linking the harness to the plough. (Ssx)

Chapman
An itinerant pedlar, hawker, or merchant; one who buys and sells; a trader.

Chare
1. *Plough Share.

2. Chair.

Charger
A large flat dish for carrying a joint of meat to the table; the largest dish in a *garnish of *pewter.

Charing Rake
Rake for separating the chaff from corn. (Dby)

Chariot
An open *carriage; a cart or waggon.

Chased
Ornamental with embossed work.

Chasuble
A priest's vestment; a sleeveless *mantle worn over the *alb and stole when celebrating mass.

Chattel
Movable possessions, including livestock; also including leasehold property - but not other types of real estate. All chattels should have been listed in probate inventories. See *Cattle.

Chattel Lease
A *lease, which could be bequeathed by will. Sometimes referred to as chattels, chattel estates, or simply *leases.

Chechyng, Chicthing
Kitchen.

Cheeks
Upright stones or irons in a fireplace; the sides of a grate.

Cheese Board, Bread
Round board placed on top of a cheese to press it down in the press.

Cheese Brig
Wooden cross bars resting on the cream pan to support the skimming bowl so that it may drip into the liquid below.

Cheese Cowl
Tub or pail in which cheese and rennet were mixed in the early stages of cheese-making.

Cheese Cratch, Heck, Racka, Vecke, Wrack
Rack for drying and storing newly made cheese.

Cheese Ladder
Support for the cheese vat to rest upon over a cheese tub whilst the whey is pressed out.

Cheese Mote
*Cheese Vat.

Cheese Press, Cheese Wring
Press used in cheese-making, to compress the curds and expel the moisture and whey.

Cheese Vat
Mould in which cheese was made. The curds are placed in it, and the cheese is shaped under a press, expelling the whey.

Chell, Chendel
Candlestick.

Cherkey
*Turkey.

Chest Bed
*Press Bedstead.

Chested
Placed in coffin.

Cheverell
Kid leather, noted for its pliability and stretching capability.

Chewtawe
*Hatchell. (Wor)

Cheyeer Mill
A shear-mill: for making either plough shares or shears.

Cheyney
1. China.
2. A printed woollen or worsted fabric, sometimes used for curtains.

Chilver
Ewe lamb.

Chimlin
*Kimnel.

Chimney
The term may refer to iron structures erected over open hearths, prior to the time when stone chimneys became common.

Chimney Board
Board used to close a chimney during the summer.

Chimney Crane
Iron implement fixed with brackets to the back of a hearth, which could be swung out to support cooking pots over the fire.

Chimney Glass
Mirror hung on a chimney breast.

Chimney Money
Hearth tax, imposed between 1662

and 1689.

Chimney Piece
Hood over the fire to channel smoke into the chimney; usually ornamental, and often associated with a shelf or mantle.

Chin Cloth
A band of cloth passing under a woman's chin; a muffler.

Chine
The backbone and adjoining flesh of a pig slaughtered for bacon. Remaining when the sides are cut off for curing.

Chintz
Painted or stained *calico imported from India, usually glazed.

Chips
Strips of wood holding fast the plough share.

Chirurgery
Surgery.

Chittle
*Kettle.

Chock, Choker
Neckerchief worn high around the throat.

Chopping Block, Stock
1. A piece of tree-trunk on which wood was chopped up.
2. A block of wood on which food was chopped up.

Chrisom, Christening Sheet
A white sheet or robe worn by babies and children at baptism; a token of innocence. If the child died within a month it was used as a shroud; otherwise it was given as an offering at the mother's churching or purification.

Christmas Box
Earthen-ware container used by servants for collecting gratuities at Christmas.

Church Work
Fabric, possibly richly embroidered, which had belonged to a pre-Reformation church, but which had been sold off and put to secular use when the reformers arrived, perhaps cut up into cushions.

Churchys
Kerchief.

Churn

A conical shaped vessel with a perforated plunger worked by an up and down motion, used to make butter from cream. Replaced by the revolving churn, which was barrel-shaped, and revolved on pivots.

Churn Staff
Wooden plunger or pale used to agitate cream in a churn in order to make butter.

Chusinett
*Cushionet.

Chymer
Loose or light gown. (Nth)

Cichin
Kitchen

Cider Mill, Press, Wring
Apples for cider were, in theory, first crushed in a cider mill, and then pressed in a cider press or wring to extract the juice. However, these terms were often used synonymously.

Cilhouse
*Gyle House.

Cine
*Kine

Cistern
1. Water container for the household, sometimes called a *lead (2) and frequently located in the kitchen.
2. Brewing vat.
3. The water tank in which grains was soaked in malting.

Cithern, Citterne
A musical instrument similar to a guitar, strung with wire, and played with a plectrum.

Cittermister
*Kidderminster Stuff.

Cives
*Keives.

Civet
An animal ranking in size between a fox and a weasel; hence a `purse of civet' is made from its fur.

Clam
Clamp, vice, or pincers, sometimes used to hold leather together for sewing.

Clapboard, Clapholt
Split oak used for wainscoting and barrel staves, etc., or for weather

boarding roofs and walls.

Clasper
Metal fastener.

Clatts
Cow dung used as fuel.

Clavichord
A small keyboard instrument with a soft tone.

Clavel, Clavy
Beam of wood serving as a lintel over the fire-place; the mantel.

Cleat
Wedge-shaped piece of wood, especially as used in securing the movable parts of ploughs and scythes.

Cleaver
1. Butcher's knife.
2. Large wooden wedge for splitting timber.

Clerk
Clergyman.

Clevis
1. Strong hooks fixed to the end of a chain or rope.
2. U-shaped piece of iron bolted to the end of a plough or wain, forming a loop to which tackle might be attached.
3. Part of the tackle of lifting gear.

Clew
A small measure of yarn, a ball.

Cliching Knife
Knife for trimming horses' hooves.

Clipes
Iron hooks in the chimney from which pots were hung. (Dur)

Cloak Bag
Travelling bag or portmanteau.

Cloam, Cloaming
Earthenware. (Dev)

Clock
Silk thread pattern on the side of stockings.

Clock Reel
Wooden device to measure the length of a skein of yarn. (Nfk; Sfk)

Clog, Clodge
Piece of wood attached to a beast to impede movement. (Dby)

Clog Chair
Chair or bench made from a thick plank or block of wood.

Clog, Clodge Wheels
Wooden cart wheels made out of planks, without spokes.

Close
1. An enclosed field.
2. Yard for cattle; farmyard.

Close Barrell, Chair, Jake, Stool
Commode or chamber pot, generally consisting of a pan or pot enclosed in a box or barrel type structure, to keep the smell in.

Close Bed
A box bed, built into the wall, and perhaps hidden behind panelling, totally enclosed and entered by sliding doors or shutters.

Close Bonk, Bounk
Bucket with a lid or cover used for washing.

Close Cart
A farm cart.

Close Hose
Close fitting hose.

Close Kit
Wooden tub for washing clothes. (Dby)

Closet
A room for storage.

Cloth Female
Fine linen. (Lin)

Cloth of Tissue
A rich cloth, often interwoven with silver or gold.

Cloth Press
Press used in the process of cloth finishing.

Clothes Hussey
Box for storing clothes. (Gls)

Clothier
A maker and/or seller of cloth.

Clout
1. A metal patch or plate used by a blacksmith for mending, and especially one fixed to an *axle tree or to parts of a plough to prevent wear by chafing.
2. A fragment, a piece.
3. A piece of cloth containing pins and needles.

Clout Leather
Thick leather for shoe soles or for patching.

Clove Bark
The spice from a species of cinnamon

tree, with the flavour of cloves.

Clove Iron
*Clevis.

Clowes
Thread wound on bobbins. (Lan)

Coal
1. Charcoal. This is likely to be the usual meaning as *sea coal was not suitable for cooking on an open hearth.
2. *Sea Coal.

Coal Rake
For raking cinders from an oven when it was hot enough to bake bread.

Coal Tankard
Coal scuttle. (Gls)

Coal Vat
Vat used to measure coal.

Coarslett
*Corselet.

Coast
Barrel holding 9 gallons, or a measure of this amount. (Dev)

Coat
1. An outer garment.
2. Petticoat.

Cobb
A small, sturdy horse.

Cobbars
Horse equipment. (Chs)

Cobard, Cobart, Cobberd
1. *Cupboard.
2. *Cobiron.

Cobiron
1. Bar with hooks which supported a spit over the hearth, used instead of *andirons. They rested at an angle at the back of the fireplace, with the spit placed on two hooks.
2. A cradle for firewood.

Coble
Open fishing boat, without deck or keel, but with sharp bows and a flat, sloping stern.

Cobweb Lawn
Very fine transparent linen fabric.

Cocer
A dealer. (Lin)

Cocher
A mattress. (Nth)

Cochineal
A brilliant red dye, made from the dried body of an insect, coccus cacti; also used medicinally.

Cock
1. Tap.
2. Small conical heap.
3. Ship's boat.

Cock and Chain
Piece of iron with notches, fixed at the end of the plough beam.

Cockloft
Space between the ceiling and the roof, reached by ladder; perhaps an attic or garret.

Cockshut Net
Net suspended between two poles for catching woodcock in flight, perhaps at twilight.

Coconut
A coconut shell cup, usually with a silver framework and lip.

Cod
Pillow or cushion.

Codware
Pillowcase.

Codbear
*Pillow Bere.

Coffer
Lockable box or chest, often with a leather-covered lid, used for the storage of clothes or valuables.

Coffin
Small chest or box.

Cog
Type of fishing boat distinctive to the Rivers Humber and Ouse. (Lin; Yks)

Cogware
Coarse cloth made of inferior wool. (Nth)

Coif
Close-fitting cap, covering the top, back and sides of the head, worn by women or clerics.

Colander
Perforated metal vessel used as a sieve or strainer.

Collar
Usually refers to the bridles or halters of horses and oxen, especially that portion through which power is directly exerted.

Collar Holster
Halter for securing a horse in a stall.

College Cup
An early form of *porringer.

Collock
A wooden tub or pail.

Colt
Horse less than five years old, but no longer a foal.

Colt Irons
Used to bind the *coulter to the frame of the plough.

Comb
1. *Card.
2. A measure of capacity; four bushels.
3. A brewing vat or tub. (Bkm)

Comfit
A sweetmeat made from fruit and sugar.

Commerce Table
Table used to play a game called `commerce', the 18th c. equivalent of Monopoly.

Commissary
Clergyman deputising for a superior authority.

Commode
1. Chest of drawers; it did not become a *close stool until the 19th c.
2. A tall head-dress of silk or lace, on a wire frame, worn by women.

Commodity
Convenience and advantage; benefit derived from landed property.

Common Field
Land owned in common by the whole community, usually divided into arable strips for individual farmers, who also had pasture rights over the whole field.

Commons
Provender, provisions.

Comparcioner
Joint owner; one who shares an inheritance or estate with another.

Compass
Compost: manure or night soil.

Compass Saw
A saw with a narrow blade which cuts circularly.

Compass Window
Semi-circular bay window.

Compast
Round.

Composition Money
Payment made in lieu of a larger amount or other obligation; a sum paid by royalists to Parliament to `compound' for their `delinquency'; a *fine.

Compter
*Counter; also the name of certain debtors' prisons.

Conduit
Pipe or channel for running water.

Confection
Medicinal preparation made from various drugs.

Cony
Rabbit; rabbit skin.

Cony Hayes
Rabbit warren.

Cony Flax
Rabbit fur.

Cool Back
Cooler, especially in a *brewhouse.

Cool House
Room in which perishables are kept cool.

Cooler
Shallow pan, staved tub or trough in which milk, *wort, or other liquids are set to cool.

Cooling Lead
Large tub for brewing.

Coop
1. A basket, probably wicker.
2. Small shed or hutch for poultry or other animals
3. A cart with closed sides and ends, suitable for carting dung, lime, etc. Probably with two wheels or perhaps mounted on sled runners.

Coop Sole
Lower supporting timber frame of a *coop (3).

Cooper
Maker of barrels and other wooden vessels made of staves and hoops.

Coopery Ware
Collective term for tubs, barrel, *keives, casks, etc., made of staves and hoops by a *cooper.

Cop
1. Cover for a waggon. (Sal)
2. The beam placed between a pair of draught oxen. (Dby)

3. The movable frame attached to the front or sides of a waggon to extend its surface when carrying bulky loads such as hay or corn.

Cope
Priest's vestment, resembling a long cloak, made from a semi-circular piece of silk or other material, without sleeves.

Coperture
A covering of fabric. (Con)

Copper
Large vessel made of copper, used for cooking or laundry purposes, or for brewing.

Copperas
Type of salt, used in dyeing, tanning, and ink-making. Also known as green vitriol, or sulphates of iron and zinc.

Copse
*Clevis (2).

Copsole
Wedge for keeping the plough's *coulter at the right angle.

Copy Book
Book in which exercises were written or printed for pupils to imitate..

Copyhold
Land held by copy of the manorial court roll, in accordance with the custom of the manor.

Corbut
Deep tub for salting meat. (Dev)

Cord
1. Cords were attached to *bedframes and made to form a tight net or web to support a rush or straw *mat and the *bed, i.e. the mattress.
2. A measure of 128 cubic feet of sawn wood.

Cord Wood
Smaller branches cut in lengths of four feet or so and stacked in `cords', for fuel and charcoal-making.

Cordovan
Fine Spanish leather made from goatskins, originally from Cordoba.

Cordwainer
Leather worker, usually a shoe-maker; originally a worker in *cordovan.

Corf, Corve
1. A basket made of hazel-rods, in which coal was carried to the surface in mines; subsequently, a waggon used for the same purpose.
2. A measure of coal.

Coriander
A plant whose seeds are used for flavouring purposes.

Corkell
Grindstone. (War)

Cornish Mat
Wall to wall rush mats to be found in the grandest rooms.

Corporal, Corporas
Linen used during the celebration of the mass to stand the bread and wine on, and to cover it.

Corr Fish
Salted fish. (Dev)

Corse
Ribbon or band, ornamented with metal-work or embroidery, and used as a *girdle or garter.

Corse Present
*Mortuary.

Corselet, Corslet
A light iron breastplate worn by foot soldiers.

Corser
A dealer, especially a horse dealer.

Corvisor
*Cordwainer.

Coster
Wall or bed *hangings (2).

Costrel
Large bottle or wooden keg, which had ears or a handle, by which it could be suspended from the waist or neck, and carried to the field or on a journey.

Cote
Small shed for pigs, sheep, hens, etc., or for storage.

Cotland
The small piece of arable land held by a cottar with his 'cot'.

Cotter
Small iron pin, key, or wedge for securing a bolt.

Cotterell
Adjustable hook, crane, or bar, for hanging pots over a fire. (Southern)

Cotton
A woollen cloth with a frizzy nap.

Couch, Couch Bed
A day bed without canopy or hangings.
Couch Chair
A backless sofa against a wall with an arm at each end; a long *settle.
Coucher
Table cloth.
Couching Floor, House
Floor or room where grain was spread to germinate in the preparation of *malt or woad.
Coulett
*Coverlet.
Coulter
A plough's iron blade, fixed in front of the share, to cut the soil vertically; the share then cuts it horizontally.
Counter, Counter Board, Counter Table
1. Desk or writing table where accounts could be prepared, money counted, etc.
2. Dresser or side-table.
Counter Beam
The bars from which the scales of a balance are suspended.
Counterfeit
Dishes made of base metal, as opposed to silver.
Counterpane, Counterpoint
A quilted *coverlet; the uppermost covering for a bed.
Counting House
Room for keeping accounts, receiving moneys, etc.
Coup
*Coop.
Couple
A ewe and a lamb together.
Course
Sails on the lower yards of a ship.
Court Cupboard
Two or three tiered sideboard, perhaps with doors to the lower tier; pewter or plate could be displayed on top, linen stored below, perhaps with more pewter.
Court Leet
Manor or hundred court, held twice yearly, concerned with minor misdemeanours, suits for debt, appointment of constables, etc.

Court Roll
Record of the business of a manorial court, kept on a roll of paper or parchment, and including much information on tenurial matters.
Courtledge
*Curtilage.
Cousin
A kinsman or woman; a term frequently applied historically to nephews or nieces, as well as to those descended from different children of common grandparents.
Covart
*Coverlet.
Covenant
An agreement between master and servant, for the latter to serve for a specified period in return for board, wages etc.
Covenant Year
A year's work agreed between master and servant at the end of the latter's apprenticeship.
Coventry Blue, Coventry Thread
Thread made in Coventry, usually blue, and used for embroidery.
Cover Fire
Cover to put over a fire to keep it burning with safety overnight.
Covered Chair
Chair with padded seat and back.
Coverings
*Coverlet.
Coverlet
The uppermost bed covering, which could be made of various materials; a quilt or *counterpane.
Covert
*Coverlet.
Coverture
The legal status of a married woman, under the authority and protection of her husband.
Covin
Fraudulent action.
Cowick
A variety of apple. (Dev)
Cowl
1. A large tub for water, usually with two ears, through which a cowl staff could be passed so that it could be

carried by two men.

2. An open tub used for cooling in brewing or butter-making, or for salting meat.

Cow Rack
Hay rack for cattle.

Coytte
1. *Coif.
2. Matted sheep's fleece used as a doormat. (Lin)

Crab Lock
Crab-shaped locks with five points for locking soft material such as money bags.

Crab Mill, Press
Mill or press for pounding or crushing crab apples in the making of cider or verjuice.

Crab Trough
Trough for making vinegar from crab apples.

Crack, Crackle
Implement for preparing hemp. (Dby; Sts)

Cracknel
Hard, crisp biscuit.

Cradle
1. Framework of bars, rods, cords, etc., for holding or protecting something.
2. A light wooden frame attached to a scythe, with a row of long curved teeth parallel to the blade, designed to ensure that the mown grass fell compactly into even swathes.

Cradle Cloth
*Swaddle bands.

Cradle Iron
A framework of bars, or a grating, supporting cooking pots beside a fire.

Crane
An iron bar fixed on a pivot in the chimney, from which pots are suspended over a fire.

Crape
A light cloth, thin worsted stuff, made in Norfolk, sometimes used for woollen shrouds, which were compulsory after 1678; also for the clothes of clergy.

Cratch
1. Storage rack or manger for animal fodder.
2. Framework from which *flitches

were suspended.
3. *Handle Cratch.

Crate
1. A hurdle.
2. Box with open bars or slots.

Crates
A pair of panniers used for carrying heavy goods on pack-horses. (Dby)

Craveth
Humbly requests.

Crayer
Small trading ship.

Crazing and Stamping Mill
Mills for crushing tin ore. (Con)

Creale, Creel
Osier basket for carrying fish. (Lin; Yks)

Crease
*Crest.

Creeper
1. Iron dogs placed between the *andirons in a grate, to support burning logs.
2. Small frying pan with three legs.

Cresse
Cloth, probably canvas, from Crécy in France.

Cresset
1. Iron container holding pitched rope, grease, or oil, to be burnt as a light; mounted on a pole or hung from the roof.
2. Device for hanging pots over a fire.
3. Small pan for boiling lead. (Dby)

Crest, Crest Tile
Tile for the ridge of a roof.

Crest, Crest Cloth
Type of linen cloth.

Crewel
1. Thin worsted yarn for embroidery or tapestry.
2. Embroidery needles.
3. Embroidery worked in wool onto linen.

Crib
1. A barred rack containing fodder for cattle to feed from; a *cratch.
2. A baby's cradle.
3. The body of a cart.

Cricket
A low foot-stool, three-legged, perhaps used when milking cows.

Crock
1. A metal pot generally of brass or iron, with three short legs and a handle from which it could be hung.
2. An earthenware pan.
3. *Crook.
4. Soot.

Crocus
Saffron, used as a yellow dye; cloth dyed with saffron.

Croft
Enclosure, usually adjacent to the dwelling house, and used for tillage or pasture.

Crok Hangings
*Hangings.

Cromb
Wooden handled rake with two long hooked prongs, used for spreading manure.

Crook
A hook, which could be of various different kinds. A pair of crooks were often hung above the hearth to support cooking utensils. Crooks might be found associated with ploughs or used to hold loads on the backs of pack-horses. Not to be confused with *crocks, although frequently with the same spelling.

Crook Steady
An iron or wooden bar in a chimney from which a crook is hung. (Dur)

Cross
1. Cross-bow; a weapon with a bow fixed on a wooden stock, with a device for holding and releasing the string.
2. Cooper's tool for cutting a groove at the end of a cask to fit the lid.

Cross Bridge
The frame at the back of a waggon which hold the side pieces in place.

Cross Cloth
1. Linen cloth worn on the forehead.
2. Knitted handkerchief. (War)

Cross Staff
Instrument for measuring the altitude of heavenly bodies.

Cross Week
Rogation week.

Crow
Bar of iron with one end slightly bent, used as a lever; a crow-bar.

Crown
English coin worth five shillings; also the French `ecu', often seen in England in the 16th c.

Crown Gold
Gold of high quality.

Crown Lace
Lace patterned with crowns, acorns and roses.

Crows
Rotatable form of *Trippet.

Cruck
Wooden pail for carrying water or milk.

Cruet
Vessel to hold wine or holy water at the celebration of the eucharist, etc.

Crum
Crooked.

Crupper
Leather strap which passed from the saddle under the horse's tail, to prevent the saddle sliding forward.

Crusado
Portuguese coin bearing the sign of the cross.

Cruse
1. Small glass bottle holding vinegar or oil, which could be poured out slowly through a narrow pipe on the side.
2. Small earthenware jar or pot, usually for drinking.

Crusk, Cruskin
Wooden or earthenware drinking-cup; pot, jar or bottle. (Dby)

Crust, Crust Board
Plank of timber from the side of a log, with bark on one side.

Cub
1. A *crib for fodder: a bin, pen or receptacle.
2. Cage or *coop(2) for poultry and other animals.
3. Young animal.

Culgee
Figured Indian silk.

Culm
Poor quality coal used in lime-burning and for drying *malt.

Culter
*Coulter.

Cumin
An umbelliferous plant grown for its seed, used in cooking.

Cup
Drinking vessel, usually of pewter or tin.

Cupboard
Board, supported by legs, and perhaps with shelves, used to store and display crockery, and especially cups; a sideboard. Easily confused with variants of *cobiron.

Cupboard Table
Side table with shelves to display silver or pewter.

Curb
1. Stand in a brewery to support a cask.
2. Framing round the top of a brewer's copper.
3. Two-handled windlass.
4. Framing around a well.

Curd Rake
Agitator used in the dairy.

Curnock
A measure of corn, usually four bushels of barley or oats, and three of wheat.

Currier
1. An early firearm.
2. A tradesman who dresses and colours leather after it has been tanned.

Curry
A small cart.

Curry Comb
Metal instrument for grooming horses.

Currying Knife
Knife used by a *currier to dress leather after tanning.

Currying Pan
A vessel for dressing (soaking or colouring) tanned hides.

Curtain
Likely to be for a *bedstead rather than a window; not used for the latter until the 18th c.

Curtal
Horse with its tail docked.

Curtilage
Small court or yard attached to a house or farm.

Cushion Stool
Stool with a padded seat.

Cushionet
A small cushion; a pin-cushion.

Cut
Sweet new wine.

Cut Work
Open-work lace or embroidery.

Cutling Tub
Tub for coarse oatmeal.

Cuttleaxe
Cutlass: a short sword with a wide, flat, slightly curved blade.

Cuttle Bone
Shell of the cuttlefish, used in polishing.

Cutwith
The cross-bar of a *plough or *harrow to which the *traces are attached.

Cyder Wring
*Apple Wring

Cypress
1. Wood from the cypress tree.
2. Various kinds of valuable textiles imported from Cyprus.

Dabbit
Couch or day-bed. (Yks)

Dabnet
1. Small fishing net for use in streams. (Oxf)
2. *Dobnet.

Daffy Elixir
Medicine containing gin, invented by Thomas Daffy, and given to infants to quiet them.

Dag
Heavy hand-gun or pistol.

Dagswain
Coarse coverlet of shaggy, rough material.

Damask
A rich silk fabric, woven with elaborate designs, originally from Damascus. Later, a twilled table linen, with an elaborate design woven in, seen by the reflection of light; the term was subsequently applied to any fabric woven in this way.

Dannock
Hedger's gloves: the left hand glove was left whole in order to grasp thorns; the right had fingers so that a bill hook

could be used.

Dansk, Dantsick
16th c. English for Denmark and Danzig; hence used of imports from the Baltic in general, especially goods made of spruce. Dansk chests sometimes incorporated marquetry work.

Dark Lantern
*Lanthorn with a shutter to hide its light.

Darnacles, Darnix
*Dornick

Dasher
Detachable upright boards on the side of a waggon to increase its capacity, and to hold the load in place. (Ntt)

Dashin
Tub for the preparation of oatmeal.

Dateler, Daytail Man
One who works by the day; not regularly employed. (Northern)

Daubing
Plasterwork; infilling of clay, dung or straw for timber-framed buildings.

Day House
Dairy.

Day Net
A small net used by day to catch larks, water fowl, and other small birds.

Day Work
Crops growing on an area of land that could be worked in one day, usually considered to be about three roods.

Dead
Inanimate goods.

Dead-Eye
Block with three holes through which a lanyard is reeved, to extend the shrouds on a sailing ship.

Deal
A plank or board no more than seven inches wide and three inches thick, usually of fir or other soft wood.

Decretal
Collection of papal decrees, forming part of canon law.

Defeasance
Collateral deed expressing a condition which, if fulfilled, renders the deed null and void.

Defender Iron
Iron fender in front of a fire.

Delf
A ditch, trench, drain, pit, or quarry, perhaps dug for the purpose of irrigation or drainage.

Delft, Delph Ware
Good quality blue and white tin glazed earthenware, of a type originally made in Delft.

Demath
A day's mowing. (Chs)

Demicastor
Felted hat, probably of beaver or other fur. (Lan)

Demiceint
Girdle with ornamental work on the front.

Demy
A short, close vest; a doublet or jacket.

Deposition
A statement or testimony made under oath in answer to interrogatories, and recorded in writing, so that it can be read in court without the presence of the witness.

Derig
*Dirige.

Desk
Portable boxes fitted with locks for writing materials, letters, etc. Legs were added at a later date, to give the *standing desk, with a sloping, hinged lid, which could be used for writing.

Desperate Debts
Debts which were unlikely to be recoverable, perhaps unsecured by *bond.

Deust Bed
*Dust Bed.

Dey, Deyhouse
Dairy. (Oxf; War)

Diachylon
Ointment made from vegetable juices, applied with linen bandages.

Dial
Surveyor's compass.

Diaper
Twilled white linen cloth woven with geometric patterns, used as towels or napkins for drying hands during meals; also used as table cloths or for other purposes. Originally made in Ypres,

Belgium; hence the name (d'Ypres).

Diaper Ring
Ring with a *diaper pattern.

Diascord, Diascordium
A medicinal powder made from the dried leaves of teucrium scordium and other herbs.

Dicker
A bundle of ten hides or skins.

Diet
Daily food; may also refer to board, or to one's way of life in general.

Dight
Dressed, prepared.

Dill
A yellow flowering herb cultivated for its carminative seeds, i.e. as a cure for flatulence.

Dimidia
One-half (Latin).

Dimity
Stout cotton fabric with raised stripes or fancy figures, used undyed mainly for bed coverings and hangings.

Dinch Pick
Three-pronged *dung fork. (Oxf)

Dintle
A thin type of leather. (Lin; Yks)

Dirige
Funeral service, from the Latin `dirige', the first word in the Latin antiphon in matins, part of the office for the dead.

Dish
The smallest dish of the pewter *garnish.

Dish Bink, Board, Cage, Cradle, Crate
Rack or dresser for storing, displaying, and perhaps drying plates and dishes.

Dish Call
*Call. (Yks)

Dish Ring
Ring on which to stand hot dishes on the table.

Diss
Type of grass from the Mediterranean, with fibrous stems used for making cords.

Distaff
Cleft stick about three feet long on which wool or flax was wound for spinning by hand.

Distraint
Taking possession of a property for the non-performance of some legal obligation.

Distress
The legal seizure of chattels in order to compel the honouring of some obligation.

Dithe
Cow dung cut and made into squares for fuel. (Lin; Yks)

Ditty
*Dimity.

Divers
More than one; an indefinite number.

Dobnet
Cooking pot or small cooking utensil.

Docion, Doshan
Vessel in which oat-meal is prepared.

Dock
The crupper of a saddle or harness.

Docking Iron
Tool for docking horses tails.

Dod
A stave or club. (War)

Dog
1. Fire-dog: bar supporting the end of a log, or on which a spit is turned in the fire-place.
2. *Andiron.
3. A type of clamp.
4. A lever for placing iron hoops on cart wheels.

Dog Iron
*Dog (1 & 2).

Dog Wheel
Treadmill operated by a dog to turn a spit.

Doggne
Dung

Dole
1. Gift to the poor.
2. Strip of meadow land, the use of which is rotated annually.
3. Share, portion, or lot, e.g. of profits from a fishing trip.

Donge
Mattress. (Nfk)

Door
Doors were legally considered to be movables, and could therefore be listed in probate inventories.

Door Band

*Band (4)

Door Piece
Curtains covering a door.

Door Tree
Door post or bar.

Dorman
The fixed end of a joined table.

Dormant Table
Table fixed to the floor in a permanent position.

Dornick
A coarse variety of *damask: a silk, woollen or worsted fabric used for *carpets and *hangings, originally made in Dornick, Belgium (Tournay in Flemish).

Dorter
Dormitory in a monastery.

Dossel, Dosser
Pannier carried by a horse.

Double Gilt
Gilded with a double coating of gold.

Doubler
A large bowl or dish, which could be of pewter, earthenware, or wood, sometimes used for making pies.

Doublet
A close fitting garment, sometimes with detachable sleeves fastened at the armholes, and worn with *hose; the typical male dress, 16-18th c.

Dough Brake
Machine for mixing and kneading dough.

Dough Cowl
Cooler, generally wooden, used in baking.

Dough Kever, Trough, Trendle
Shallow circular tray or trough in which dough was mixed before baking.

Doules
A nail sharpened at each end to fasten planks. (War)

Dovetail Joint
Tenon joint shaped like a dove's tail, to fit a mortice of that shape.

Dow, Dowed
Dull, faded, perhaps reddish-brown.

Dower
The portion of a husband's estate allowed to his widow for life.

Dowl, Down
Soft feathers used to fill the highest quality mattresses and pillows.

Dowlais
A coarse linen or *calico used by the poor for sheets, skirts, smocks, etc. Originally from Daoules or Doulas, in Brittany.

Down
Soft feathers used for stuffing *beds etc.

Dozens
Type of *kersey; coarse woollen cloth. (Dev)

Drab
Un-dyed thick woollen cloth.

Draff Tub
Tub for the refuse or grains of *malt after brewing.

Draft Rake
A large rake for corn or hay.

Drag
1. A heavy harrow for breaking up ground.
2. Sledge for transporting heavy objects.
3. Type of brake.
4. Butcher's hook.
5. Implement used in the hearth.

Drag Corn
Oats and barley sown together.

Dragon, Dragoon
A type of *carbine, so-called because it appeared to `breathe fire' like a dragon.

Drall
*Thrall.

Dram Dish
Dish for serving small amounts of spirits or hot drinks.

Drape
1. Cloth, drapery; originally woollen cloth.
2. Sheep or cow being fattened for slaughter, especially one which has ceased to give milk.

Drast
A privy.

Draught
1. A team of oxen or horses with their cart or plough.
2. Shaft of a *wain or cart.
3. A sledge. (Dor)

3. A measure of wool. (Oxf)

Draught Hook
Used for pulling heavy weights.

Draught Net
Fishing net.

Draught Yoke
*Yoke.

Draw Bed
An extending bed. (Lin)

Drawer
Tool for drawing out nails.

Drawers
Male undergarment for the lower body.

Drawing Knife
1. Carpenter's tool for shaving and
smoothing wood, consisting of a blade
set at right angles to two handles,
drawn towards the carpenter in use.
Also used by farriers.
2. Knife for disembowling carcasses.

Draw Table, Drawing Table
Extending table made with three
leaves, the outer two sliding under
the middle one when not in use; it
may also have a drawer or cupboard
underneath.

Drawn Work
Fabrics ornamented by drawing out
threads of the warp and woof to form
patterns, perhaps also with needle-
work.

Dray
1. *Sled.
2. Plough made without wheels or
feet.
3. Cart without sides used by brewers.

Dray Blades
Wooden slats beneath a *dray or
sledge.

Dreap
Barren. (Yks)

Dredge
1. A mixture of grains (usually oats
and barley) sown together, sometimes
malted for brewing.
2. An inferior barley.

Dredger, Dredging Box
Box with a perforated top for
sprinkling, e.g., salt, flour, sugar, etc.

Drench Vat
Container in which skins are steeped.

Dresser

1. A table or flat board for preparing
food, dressing meat, or displaying
plate or pewter; subsequently, a chest
of drawers with shelves on top for
displaying pewter.
2. Any implement or utensil used
to dress or prepare objects, e.g. a
shoemaker's tool for preparing leather.

Dresser Board
*Dresser

Dressing Beam
Work bench.

Dressing Board
1. Board on which cloth is laid to raise
the nap.
2. *Dresser.

Dressing Box
Box for toilet accessories, often with a
small mirror.

Drift
1. Drove way for cattle.
2. Fishing net.
3. Ramming tool.

Drink Can
A cylindrical vessel, not necessarily of
metal, for holding drink.

Drink Stall
A wooden stand for holding tubs, etc.,
of drink.

Dripping Broach
Spit.

Dripping Pan
Pan placed under a *spit to catch drips
from the meat.

Drug Saw
Cross-cut saw.

Drugget
A coarse woollen material, or perhaps
mixed with linen or silk, felted or
woven, sometimes printed on one side,
and used for *wearing apparel, or for
table or floor coverings.

Dry
Barren, when it refers to animals.

Dry Hair
*Hair Cloth.

Dry Vat, Vessel
Container for corn, meal, and other
dry goods.

Dubbing Board
Board for dressing cloth.

Dublas

*Dowlais

Ducape
Plainly woven, stout silk fabric, introduced by Huguenot refugees in 1685.

Ducat
A gold coin in circulation throughout Europe, of varying value.

Duch Canvas
A strong untwilled linen cloth.

Dudgeon Dagger
Dagger with a hilt made of dudgeon, a common box-wood.

Dudger
Basket. (Gls)

Dulcimer
A musical instrument; its strings are stretched over a trapezoidal sounding board, and struck by two hand-held hammers.

Dumb Waiter
Serving trolley on wheels, resembling cake-stands, often of three tiers.

Dun
Brown or greyish brown; a term often applied to horses.

Dung Fork, Hook
Fork with crooked prongs for manure spreading.

Dung Cart
Heavy two-wheeled cart for carrying manure to the fields, perhaps with detachable shafts, and able to tip.

Dung Crib
1. *Dung Cart.
2. *Dung Pot.

Dung Pot
*Pannier with door at the bottom which could be strapped to a horse's back, used for carrying dung to the fields.

Durance
A strong, durable cloth.

Duroy
Common type of coarse woollen fabric. (Dev)

Dust Bed
Mattress filled with chaff.

Dutch Chair
A ladder back, rush-seated chair.

Eager

Sour or tart, especially of beer or wine.

Eander
*Andiron

Ear
1. The handle of a dish or pot.
2. The part of a bell by which it is hung.

Ear Picker
An instrument for cleaning wax from the ear.

Earth
Made of earthenware.

Earwingle, Erwing
*Windle Blade. (Sal)

Easement
The right to use that which is not one's own, e.g. a right of way.

East Cloth
Cloth from the Baltic, i.e. the Eastland.

Easter Book
A rector or vicar's book for recording Easter dues.

Eatage
Grass available only for grazing, especially the growth after hay has been cut.

Eatherhead
*Netherhead

Ech, Eche Hook
Hook on a cart or waggon which a rope passes through to hold its load in place.

Ecuelle
A two-handled *porringer used for soup.

Eddish
The second crop of grass, or the grass that grows on the stubble.

Edge Grain
1. Grain that ripens irregularly due to damage by bad weather.
2. Grain sown on headlands.

Edge Tool
Sharp-edged metal cutting tools such as axes, scythes, bills, etc.

Eel Spear
Two-pronged spear for catching eels by transfixing them as they lie in the mud.

Elbow Chair
Chair with two arm rests.

Elden, Elding
Fuel, brushwood, peat, etc., for

kindling fires. (Lin; Yks)

Elecampane
The horse heal, a plant with bitter leaves and roots, and very large yellow flowers, used medicinally as a stimulant.

Elect
One chosen by God for eternal salvation; the term used in wills usually signifies a Calvinistic belief in predestination.

Electuary
A medicinal paste or conserve, mixed with honey, jam or syrup.

Ell, Eln
A measure of length: generally 45 inches, although this did vary; often used to measure cloth.

Ell Father
Fore-father, grandfather, or father in law. (Dur)

Elledge
A fluid measure. (Ham)

Elsin
A shoe-maker's awl, including its blade and haft or handle.

Elting Tub
Tub for kneading dough.

End
A measure of hops. (Wor)

End Iron
*Andiron (2).

Engrain
To dye a crimson or scarlet colour with cochineal.

Entail
The right to property settled on several people in succession, so that none of them have absolute ownership - and hence the property cannot pass out of the family.

Enterclose
A partition or screen dividing up a building. (Dev)

Entremet
Side dish.

Entry
Passage inside the front door.

Entry Fine
Lump sum paid to the lord by a copyholder or leaseholder on entering his land at the beginning of a new tenancy.

Epergne
Central ornament for a dining table, usually silver, perhaps holding pickles.

Erning Gallows
Swinging *gallow tree. (Ntt)

Escript
A written document; probably referring to deeds and muniments.

Escritoire
Writing desk containing stationery and documents, often portable.

Escutcheon
Shield or *hatchment, etc. on which a coat of arms is depicted.

Eshin
Basin or *ewer for water or milk, perhaps made of ash wood. (Chs; Lan)

Estemenes
Type of woollen cloth. (Dev)

Etch
*Eddish.

Evell, Evill
A three pronged fork; a type of dung fork. (Con, Dev)

Ewer
Pitcher with a wide spout, particularly for water carrying, often used with a basin for washing.

Exe
Axe.

Exhibition
Grant to a university student.

Extinguisher
A hollow conical cap for extinguishing candles.

Eye
*Eythe.

Eye Wedge
Small wedge for securing cart wheels when their iron rim was being put in place; or perhaps for securing the back of a cart.

Eythe
Harrow.

Faced Cloth
A woollen cloth with a smooth nap.

Fages
Remnant. (Wor)

Faggot
Bundle of sticks bound together for

the fire.

Falchion
Broad sword, curved with the edge on the convex side; subsequently a sword of any kind.

Falling Band
Band or collar worn flat around the neck, or a woman's veil.

Falling Board, Table
Table which could be extended by putting up hinged flaps supported by movable gate-legs, i.e. drop-leaf, or, alternatively, which was hinged to the wall, against which it lay flat when not in use.

Fallings
*Hangings (2); *valance.

Fallow
A pale-brownish or reddish yellow.

False Raves
Boards or rails added to the side of a cart to enable larger loads to be carried.

Fan
A flat, fan-shaped wicker basket, or perhaps a specially designed wooden shovel, used in winnowing; subsequently, a mechanical device for generating a draught to separate the grain from the chaff.

Farandine
Fabric of silk and wool or hair; a dress of this material.

Fardel
1. A small bundle or parcel.
2. The fourth part of anything, e.g. especially land.

Farm
Amount due annually as rent or tax; may be applied to tithes, fines, etc., as well as land.

Farthing
1. *Fardel (2).
2. A quarter of a penny.

Farthingale
A framework of hoops, used to extend the skirts of a lady's dress so that they stood out from the waist. Fashionable in the 16th c.

Fash Tub
Mixing tub. (Dur)

Fat

*Vat or tub.

Faucet
Stopper or screw-top for the vent hole in a cask; a beer tap.

Feal Heap
Spoil tip. (Sal)

Feather Bed
Mattress filled with feathers.

Fee
Inheritable land held from a superior lord to whom homage and service is rendered.

Fee Simple
Freehold tenure.

Fee Tail
Entailed estate.

Feele Bedstead
Bed with curtains hanging from a central point above to form a canopy. (Dev)

Fell
Skin of an animal, including its hair or wool.

Felloe
Curved wooden section of a spoked wheel.

Fellow
A servant. (Sfk)

Felt
Felt hat.

Fender
Fire guard, preventing the cinders spreading from the hearth onto the floor.

Fennel
A fragrant herb cultivated for its use in sauces.

Fenestral
Small window, often fitted with paper, cloth or canvas rather than glass.

Fenugreek
A leguminous plant, whose seeds are used by farriers, and whose leaves are eaten by both animals and men.

Feoffee
Trustee invested with a freehold estate in land for charitable or other purposes.

Ferret
Stout cotton or silk tape, used for garters, etc., often decorated.

Fest

To bind an apprentice. (Yks)

Festoon
Curtains suspended between two points so that they curve gently.

Fetters
*Horse Lock.

Fewster
Maker of saddle trees. (Dby)

Feying Cloth
*Winnowing Cloth. (Lin; Yks)

Feying Rake
Rake for spreading manure or collecting rubbish. (Dby)

Fidd Hammer
A tool sharp at one end to splice a rope, with a hammer at the other end. (Dur)

Field Bed
1. Bedstead with curtains hanging from a central point, forming a canopy, and covering the framework entirely with curtains and draperies.
2. Folding bedstead which could be folded up for travelling.

Figuretto
A costly flowered material, perhaps woven with metallic threads.

Filigree
Decorated with thread and bead-work, usually of gold and silver.

Fill
*Thill.

Fillet
Head band or tape suitable for binding the hair.

Filleting
Narrow ribbon or tape.

Filosella
Worsted cloth of silk and wool.

Fimble
The male hemp plant (formerly thought to be the female plant), which produces a weaker and shorter fibre than *carl hemp, and was used for making fine linen.

Finched
Having a white streak along the back.

Finding
Maintenance for a minor, a widow, or other dependent person.

Fine
1. *Entry fine.

2. Fee paid by a tenant to transfer or alienate his land, or for some other privilege.

Firdeal
Plank of pine or fir, usually about 6 feet long, 9 inches wide and 3 inches thick.

Fire Box
Tinder box.

Fire Curtain
Fire guard or screen.

Fire Dog
*Andiron.

Fire Elden
*Elden.

Fire Fork
A two-pronged tool with a long handle which could be used as a poker, or to put fuel on the fire.

Fire House
Heated room, with perhaps the only hearth in the house, and therefore the main room.

Fire Irons
Collective term for iron implements used in the hearth.

Fire Pan
1. *Chafer.
2. Iron pan placed under a grate to catch the ashes.

Fire Pike, Prong
A long poker used in the hearth.

Fire Scummer
Fire shovel for removing ashes.

Fire Skase
Brass or copper hood with handle at the top, placed over a fire at night to allow it to burn without endangering the house.

Fire Slice
Fire shovel, perhaps used for extracting the ashes from a baking oven; its end was shaped like a spade or paddle.

Firkin
Small cask for liquids, butter, fish, etc., half a *kilderkin or a quarter of a *barrel.

Firth Timber
Brush or hedge wood or wattles. (Dev)

Fish Garth
Enclosure or weir for keeping fish in a river or pond.

Fish Kettle
Shallow oval dish, with a lid, for boiling fish.

Fisken
Rough basket. (Lan)

Fitchew
Pole cat, or weasel, and hence its fur or skin.

Flacket
1. Small flask or barrel, holding about three pints, used to carry drink to or by field workers.
2. *Flasket.

Flag
Rush, reed or coarse grass; rush or wicker-work.

Flageolet
A small wind instrument with the mouthpiece at one end, six principal holes, and, sometimes, keys.

Flagon
Large vessel with a narrow neck for holding wine or other liquors for use at table.

Flail
Implement for threshing corn by hand.

Flake
1. *Flitch.
2. A wattle hurdle, sometimes used as a temporary gate.
3. A rack hung from the ceiling to suspend *flitches or bread, etc.

Flaming
Red flannel, used for bedding and underclothes. (Dev)

Flanders Chest, Cupboard
Oak chest or cupboard carved and ornamented in the Flanders style.

Flannell
An open woollen stuff of loose texture, usually without nap.

Flask
Container of leather, metal or horn, perhaps for carrying gunpowder or liquid.

Flasket
1. *Flacket.
2. Shallow basket, with a handle at each end, used for carrying clothes.
3. A tub for washing clothes in, or for clothiers to size their warp.

Flat
Broad, shallow basket or metal dish, for carrying produce to market, or for laying out food on the table.

Flat Candlestick
Candlestick with a flat base and short stem, suitable for a bedroom.

Flat Iron
Solid metal smoothing iron, heated beside the fire.

Flat Piece
Shallow drinking cup.

Flaught
Turf sod dried and used as fuel. (Yks)

Flaxam
Similar to *buckram, but made from flax. (Chs)

Fleach
A plank cut from the outside of a tree trunk.

Fleache, Fleake, Fleek
*Flitch.

Fleam
Farrier's lancet used for blood-letting.

Flemish Stick
A measurement of cloth.

Flesh
Meat.

Flesh Axe
Meat chopper.

Flesh Barrel, Bucket, Fat, Kit, Tub
Container for salting meat for preservation.

Flesh Crook, Fork, Hook
Hook from which *flitches were suspended, or which could be used to take meat out of a pot or cauldron.

Flesh Pick, Pike
A long fork for handling hot meat.

Fletcher
A maker of, or dealer in, arrows.

Flew
A small fishing net.

Flint Glass
Lead crystal glass.

Flitch
The side of an animal, usually bacon, sometimes beef, salted and cured, and frequently `hung from the roof'.

Flitting Tye
Stake for tethering animals.

Float
1. A broad shallow vat used for cooling

in brewing.

2. Plasterer's tool for levelling the surface of plaster.

Flock
Woollen refuse used for stuffing pillows, mattresses and cushions; also used to make a poor quality cloth.

Flock Bed
Mattress filled with *flock.

Flocket
Loose garment with long sleeves.

Fly Boat
A fast sailing vessel used for the rapid transportation of goods in the coastal trade, usually flat-bottomed, and between 200 and 600 tons in weight.

Fly Leg Table
Table with a flap supported by a movable leg.

Fly Table
Table with a flap supported by a fly rail or swinging bracket.

Focer
*Forcer.

Fog
The second crop of hay, or the grass which grows up after the first crop has been harvested.

Foins
Clothing or trimmings made of the fur of the beech-marten, the polecat, the weasel, and similar animals.

Fold Bar
*Fold Pike. (Ntt)

Fold Course
Area over which a flock of sheep could be grazed; a sheep walk.

Fold Flake
*Flake (2).

Fold Pike
Staff with an iron point, used to pierce the ground in making hurdles. (Lin; Yks)

Fold-up Bed
Folding bed, probably used by servants or children.

Folding Table
Table with a hinged leaf which rested on the other leaf when not in use.

Foldstead
Fold.

Folkes Chamber

A servants' room.

Folling
Cleaning and thickening cloth by beating and washing using fuller's earth.

Follower
1. That part of a cider or cheese press by which pressure is applied
2. Foals or calves dependant on their mothers, and hence `followers'

Foot
1. An ale warmer; metal utensil that could be thrust into the fire.
2. A measure used in selling meat.

Foot Pace
1. *Carpet or mat. (Lin)
2. Platform or step; foot rest.

Foot Teams
A short chain connected to a plough or harrows.

Forcelet, Forcet,
Small chest used for storing documents, jewellery, etc.

Forcer
1. A small chest, coffer, or casket, sometimes covered with leather, bound with iron bands, and with a lock, used for the storage of documents, jewellery, and other valuables.
2. The plunger of a water pump.

Forcing Shears
Implement for clipping the upper layers of a fleece.

Fore Hammer, Forchamer
Large blacksmith's hammer; sledge hammer.

Fore House, Fore Room
The principal or front room of a house.

Fore Plane
Plane used to prepare wood for the smooth plane.

Forehead Cloth
Band worn by ladies on the forehead.

Forest Bill
A woodman's *bill.

Forest Work
Cross stitch embroidery on *canvas, depicting trees.

Forkes
Frame of a pack saddle.

Form

1. Bench without back support.
2. A stand for barrels. (Wor)

Former
Gouge, used by carpenters and
masons.

Forprised
Reserved.

Forthbringing
The carrying of a body to burial.
(Northern)

Fortle Boat
A small inshore fishing boat, crewed by
two to four men, and propelled by oars
or perhaps a small sail. (Sfk)

Fossard, Fosser, Fossett
*Forcer.

Fostler
*Forcelet

Fother
1. Fodder.
2. Standard weight of lead or stone.
3. A load or large quantity of
something, e.g. hay, wood. (Lin/Yks)

Fotheram
The space behind the rack in a stable
where hay is stored. (Dby)

Fountain
Receptacle for water or oil.

Fowling Piece
A long-barrelled gun for shooting
game, with a narrow bore for greater
accuracy.

Fowmared
Polecat. (Yks)

Frail
1. A rush basket, used for carrying
tools and meals to work.
2. *Flail.

Frame
The legs and cross-rails of a table or
bed; a supporting structure.

Frame Chair
Chair on a frame, as opposed to a box.

Frame Lace, Lacework
Lace made on a frame.

Frame Saw, Framing Saw
Saw stretched in a frame to make it
taut.

Framed Bed
Bedstead with panelled foot, head, and
possibly top; see also *Frame.

Framed Table
A joined table, with the top fixed to its
legs, stretchers, and top rails, rather
than sitting on trestles.

Frampot
Large pot used to collect vegetables
from the field. (Chs)

Frandel
A quarter of an acre. (Gls)

Frankincense
An aromatic gum resin obtained from
various different trees - fir, pine, etc.,
used for burning as incense.

Frate Hoop
Iron hoops for a barrel or tub. (Bkm)

Frater
Refectory in a monastery.

Freehold
A tenure in which the tenant holds
his land virtually absolutely in his
own right, although there may be a
notional lord.

Freelage
1. The freedom of a borough. (Dur)
2. A heritable property. (Dur)

Freestone
Stone such as limestone or sandstone
that can be cut or sawn freely in any
direction without breaking.

Freith
Wattle or brushwood for fencing.
(Dev)

French Barley, French Wheat
Buck wheat, grown for animal fodder.

French Bedstead
Bed with a wooden framework; the
corner posts were joined by rods on
which the *hangings (2) were hung.

French Hood
A hood worn at the back of the head,
but curving forward over the ears.
Fashionable in the mid-16th c.

French Teston
A silver coin, struck in France by
Francis I (1515-47).

Fret
1. Ornamental network of jewels and
flowers.
2. Wicker basket.
3. Iron hoop around the hub of a
wheel. (Dby)

Frieze
Thick, coarse woollen cloth with nap

on one side, used for outer garments.

Friezeadow
Silk plush; a fine kind of *frieze.

Frill
A small *ruff.

Fringe
Ornamental border consisting of a
narrow band with threads of silk, etc.,
attached, either loose or formed into
tassels or twists.

Frith
1. Land with sparse trees or
underwood; a plain between woods;
unused pasture land.
2. Young whitethorn, used for sets in
hedges.

Fritter Pan
Used for cooking fritters, or small
pancakes with apples in them.

Frizado
A fine kind of *frieze.

Frog
1. An oven fork or poker; a ratchet.
(Lin; Yks)
2. Small *andiron.

Frommard
Wood-worker's tool for splitting and
quartering wood. Similar to a *cleaver
(2), but smaller and with a handle.

Frontlet
Ornament or band worn on the
forehead.

Frost
Silver grey colour.

Frundle
A dry measure: two pecks. (Lin)

Frychen
Pole cat.

Frying Pan
Designed with either long handles to
enable the user to stay well clear of the
fire, or with small rings so that it could
be supported by pot *hangings.

Fuezee
A light musket or firelock.

Fuller
1. One who finishes cloth.
2. A blacksmith's tool for grooving
iron. (Oxf)

Fullers Earth
Clay used for cleansing and de-greasing
cloth.

Fulling
The process of beating cloth to clean
and thicken it.

Fume Pan
*Perfuming Pan.

Furgon
Poker. (Lin)

Furnace
*Cauldron, originally hung over an
open fire, but later set in masonry
with its own fire; used for boiling or
brewing.

Furniture
Usually used as a general term to
describe something set up for use, e.g.
a horse's harness, a bed with all its
coverings, a table with its *frame, and
so on. Hence `furnished', set up with
all that goes with it.

Fur, Furse
Furze or gorse, used as fuel.

Furrour
Blanket of fur. (Nth)

Fustian
A coarse fabric made from a mixture
of cotton and linen, with a silky finish,
used for furnishings and heavy clothes;
conjecturally originating in Fostat,
Egypt.

Fustic
Two types of wood, both of which give
a yellow dye.

Futs
Phates: a measure of brine used at
Droitwich.

Gaberdine
1. Cotton or silk material with a
woollen lining.
2. A coarse loose frock or smock.

Gabert
*Cobiron. (Oxf)

Gable Rope
A large thick rope; a cable. (Dby)

Gack
*Jack.

Gad
1. Goad: a sharp pointed rod for
driving oxen.
2. A bar of iron. (Dby)
3. A strip of open pasture, 6½ feet
wide. (Lin)

Gaff
Staff with an iron hook used by fishermen.

Gaffell, Gaffe Bow
A steel lever used for bending a cross-bow.

Gage
1. Pledge or deposit to ensure that a particular action is performed, usually financial in nature.
2. Quart pot or bowl.
3. A measure of hay, or small load carried by a pack animal. (Dby)

Gait
*Gate.

Gale
A bull or boar castrated after reaching maturity. (Dor)

Gales
*Gallows.

Gall
1. Ox gall, used in painting and pharmacy.
2. An excrescence from the leaves and young twigs of the oak, induced by insect activity, and used to make ink and tannin, as well as in medicines and in dyeing.
3. Gosling; small species of duck.

Gallery
Landing or passage.

Gallibank
*Gallows.

Galligaskins
Loose breeches or hose.

Gallipot
Small, glazed, earthenware pots used by apothecaries for ointments and medicines.

Gallon
Standard measure of capacity.

Galloon
Narrow, close-woven ribbon or braid of gold, silver or silk thread, used to trim clothes or upholstery.

Gallow Baulk
The iron cross bar in a chimney from which *crooks hung.

Gallow Crook, Hook
*Crook used on a *gallow tree.

Gallow Tree
Iron frame used to suspend pots above the hearth. Gallows were placed on either side of the hearth and could be made to swing into the required position.

Galloway
Breed of small strong horses originating in Galloway.

Gallows
1. *Gallow Tree.
2. Braces used for supporting breeches.

Galosh
Wooden clog, shoe or sandal, sometimes with leather uppers.

Gamash
Leggings or gaiters to protect the leg from being spattered with mud.

Gambadoes
Boot-like attachments to a horse's saddle to protect the rider's legs and feet from wet and cold.

Gambrel
Hook or forked stick used by butchers for hanging meat.

Gang
A set, e.g. of wheels, *felloes, harrow teeth, etc.

Gantry
Four-footed wooden stand for barrels.

Garble
Refuse from spices.

Garde Room
Lavatory or privy, with a wooden or stone seat, and a shute to ground level.

Gardeviance
Small chest for holding valuables; also a safe for meat.

Garietes
Leg armour; *greaves (2). (Ntt)

Garled
Mottled, specked, spotted.

Garn
1. Provisions.
2. Yarn, i.e. spun fibre ready for knitting or weaving.

Garner
Chest, storehouse, or small barn for grain or flour; a granary.

Garnish
Set of table vessels - *saucers, dishes, plates and *chargers - made of *pewter; usually twelve of the first

three items.

Garret
Attic; room just under the roof, usually used for storage.

Garth
Enclosed garden or yard, usually beside a house or other building.

Garye, **Gerys**
A horse or ox in a working team. (Nth)

Gaskins
*Galligaskins.

Gassloch
*Gaveloch.

Gate
Right to graze an animal on the common pasture.

Gathering Tub
Mash tun in which *malt is added to brew beer; *mashing fat.

Gaubert
The iron rack in a chimney supporting *pot crooks.

Gaud
Ornamental trinket; originally one of the larger, more ornamental beads between a decade of aves in a pair of *beads.

Gauger
Measuring instrument.

Gavelock
Iron crowbar or lever; large fork; a spear.

Gawn
1. A gallon.
2. A ladle or pail holding half a gallon.

Gayle
*Gallow Tree.

Gear
Equipment, especially horse or ploughing tackle, but sometimes used as a collective noun for a variety of different things, including livestock.

Gears
1. A general term for the apparatus of carts, mills, ploughs, harness, etc.
2. The small wires through which the warp is passed on the loom to separate the threads, so that the *shuttle containing the *weft could pass between alternate threads of the warp.

Geason, Gest
Barren, unproductive. (Bdf)

Geld
Barren.

Gelding
A castrated animal, especially a horse.

Gelt Sheep
Castrated sheep.

Gemel, Gimmal
Finger-ring that could be divided into two or perhaps three.

Gemew
1. Hinge.
2. Jaws of a bag opening on pins at both sides.

Genny
Guinea fowl; turkey.

Gentleman
A man with independent means, perhaps with the right to bear heraldic arms.

Genytes
*Adze.

Gergar
A small piece of iron. (Sry)

Gesse
*Girse.

Ghostly Enemy
The devil.

Ghostly Father
Father confessor.

Gib
Stand for a barrel. (Dev)

Gib Crook
Hook for hanging meat.

Gibbet
*Gallow Tree.

Gig
1. A winnowing fan.
2. A light, two wheeled, one-horse carriage.

Gig Mill Wheel
Rotating barrel or drum, to which teazle heads were fixed. The barrel was rotated at high speed, whilst cloth was pulled under it in the opposite direction thus raising the nap on the cloth.

Gill
Measure equal to one quarter, or, in the north, one half of a pint; vessel to hold this quantity.

Gill Pot, Vat
Pot or vat to hold a *gill of liquid.

Gilt
1. Young female pig about to give birth to its first litter.
2. Overlaid with a thin coating of gold.

Gilt Leather
Calfskin, faced with tin foil and glazed with a yellow varnish.

Gimlin
Wide but shallow tub for salting bacon. (Ntt; Yks)

Gimmer
1. Young female sheep. (Dur; Yks)
2. *Gemew .

Gimp
1. *Camlet.
2. A type of mohair.
3. Coarse lace on a wire or twine foundation, used for trimming *wearing apparel.

Gimp Lace
The coarser thread which forms the outline of the design in lace-making.

Gin
1. A machine or mechanical contrivance.
2. Horse operated device for hoisting or pumping in a pit.

Gingerline
A reddish-violet colour, from the French `zinzolin'.

Ginniel
*Jemmel.

Girandole
An elaborate *sconce ; chandeliers.

Girdle
1. A belt or chain worn around the waist in order to secure or to confine clothes, often with long ends hanging down, and sometimes used to carry a purse or a sword.
2. *Griddle.

Girdler
Maker of girdles and belts.

Girse, Girth
1. Horse-girth: the leather band securing a saddle or pack on a horse's back.
2. Saddle cloth. (South West)

Girth
1. A leather or cloth band tied tightly around a horse's body to secure a saddle or pack.

2. Webbing laid across the frame of a *bedstead.

Girth Tub
Hooped barrel.

Girts
Coarsely ground oats. (Dev)

Gist
The right to pasture cattle; *agistment. (Lin; Yks)

Githern, Gitter(n)
*Cithern

Gladdin
A type of flannel. (Chs)

Glade Net
Net used for snaring birds in a glade. (Chs)

Glaive
A weapon; the term was applied at various times to lances, *bills, *halberts and swords.

Glass
Looking Glass.

Glass Box, Case, Cupboard
Storage furniture for glass-ware, hung on the wall and usually open, or perhaps with a glass front.

Glazing Wheel
Wheel coated with abrasive material, used by cutlers for sharpening knives.

Glebe
Land assigned to the support of parochial incumbents, as part of their benefice.

Glede
Sandy-grey colour. (Yks)

Gloom
Anvil. (Ess)

Go Cart
Child's cart or frame on castors, used to teach toddlers to walk.

Gobbard, Gobert
*Cobiron.

Gobbet
A piece.

Goblet, Gobnet
Drinking cup of wood, pewter, silver, etc., bowl-shaped and without handles; sometimes mounted on a foot and fitted with a cover.

Goddard, Godward
*Goblet

Goaf, Goff

A quantity of hay and corn stored in one bay of a barn. (Nfk)

Golbert
*Gaubert

Gold
Textiles made of gold thread.

Gold Weights
Scales for weighing gold.

Goodman
Courtesy term for men of substance beneath the rank of the gentry.

Goodwife, Goody
Female equivalent of *Goodman; the mistress of a house.

Goose Pan
Dripping pan; large stewing or cooking pan.

Gore
A *butt (4) that is pointed at one end; a wedge-shaped piece of land on the side of an irregular open field.

Gorget
1. Throat armour; steel collar.
2. An article of female dress covering the throat.

Gorse Hook
*Bill for cutting gorse or furze.

Gossip
God-parent; a familar acquaintance.

Goule, Gowl
1. Payment to a superior. (Oxf)
2. A quantity of corn that can be made into a sheaf. (Oxf)

Gourge
Chisel with a concave blade, used for cutting rounded grooves in wood. (Chs)

Gouty Chair
Chair with a leg rest, for sufferers from gout.

Gown
Garment with a large fur collar, which could be short or long. It was open at the front, often with pleats at front and back. Similar to an academic gown.

Gradual, Grail Book
Book containing antiphons to be sung between the epistle and the gospel at the eucharist.

Grafting Saw
Hand saw used for grafting.

Grain

1. Scarlet grain or cochineal; the dye from either of these, or dye in general; the texture of a garment.
2. Outer side of a piece of leather.
3. Seed from West Africa used as a spice and in medicine.
4. Refuse of *malt after brewing, fed to swine or cattle.
5. Acorn.

Grain Staff
Fork on a stick.

Grainer, Graining Knife
Tool used by tanners and skinners for stripping hair from hides.

Grape
Dung fork. (Dur)

Grapper
Grappling hook; a nautical term.

Grat
1. *Bread Brake.
2. *Gridiron.

Grate
Framework of iron bars holding the fuel in a fire-place.

Grave
1. Manorial officer. (Yks)
2. Spade for breaking up coarse land. (Yks)

Graver
Engraving tool.

Gray Pleyn
A type of cloth (Bdf)

Great Bible
Usually refers to Coverdale's translation of 1535.

Great Chair
Armchair with a carved, panelled back.

Greave
1. Brushwood.
2. Armour for the leg below the knee.

Greaves
The offal of rendered tallow.

Gredel
*Gridiron.

Green Copperas
The proto-sulfate of iron or ferrous sulfate, also called green vitriol, used in dyeing, tanning, and making ink.

Green Ginger
Undried root of ginger.

Green Hide
Untreated animal hide, before

tanning.

Green Sauce
Sauce made from herbs, eaten with meat.

Gressum
Entry fine paid on entering copyhold or leasehold property. (Yks)

Grey Pea
The common pea.

Grice, Gris
The fur of any grey animal.

Griddle
*Gridiron.

Gridiron
An iron grate or framework of bars, square or circular, with short legs and a long handle, for broiling food over an open fire.

Grinding Stone, Grindstone, Grindlestone
Millstone, for grinding corn or perhaps minerals.

Grintern
Place to store threshed corn; compartment in a granary. (Dor)

Gripyard
A platting of stakes and twisted boughs filled with earth to confine a water-course. (Chs)

Grise
*Girse.

Grist
Corn about to be ground, or when it has just been ground.

Grist Mill
Mill for grinding corn.

Groaning Chair
Chair for the nursing mother to sit on when receiving visitors after child-birth.

Groat
Silver coins worth four pence issued between 1351 and 1662.

Groats, Grots
Hulled and crushed grain, especially oats.

Grograin, Grogram
Thick coarse fabric of mohair, wool, and sometimes silk; often stiffened with gum.

Gromwell
Seed used medicinally.

Groove
A mine-pit or shaft.

Ground Rack
Rack for dung.

Groundsill
Horizontal timber used as a foundation for a wall.

Growings
Land let out for agricultural purposes. (Gls)

Growle Stand
A barrel used for the fermentation of *malt. (Lan)

Grubber
A large harrow; tool for grubbing up the ground.

Guard
Ornamental border or trimmings on clothing.

Gudgeon
A pivoted axle; the socket in which a rudder moves.

Guile
*Gyle.

Guinea
An English gold coin, first struck in 1663 for trading with Guinea, on the West African coast, from metal imported from thence; originally worth 20s, but from 1717, 21s.

Gum Arabic
Gum obtained from acacia, used medicinally.

Gum Dragon
Tragacanth: gum from the astragulus, used medicinally.

Gun Flagon
Large ale flagons, frequently made of pewter.

Gurgeons
Coarse meal; the coarse refuse from flour. (War)

Gyle
1. The quantity of liquor that is brewed at one brewing.
2. *Wort in the process of fermentation.

Gyle Fat, Tun, Vat
Vat which holds the *wort whilst fermenting, after the yeast has been added.

Gyle House

Brewhouse.

Haaf Net
A fishing net set with stakes to catch
the fish in the ebbing tide.

Haberdyne
Dried salt cod.

Hack
1. Mattock, pick-axe, or large hoe.
2. Rack for drying cheeses or holding
fodder.
3. Horse let out for hire.

Hackaber, Hack Hammer
Blacksmith's hammer. (Oxf)

Hackbut
*Harquebus.

Hacking Horse
*Hackney.

Hackle
Metal comb for splitting the fibres
of hemp and flax, and making them
straight and smooth.

Hackney
Horse of medium size and quality used
for ordinary riding; perhaps a lady's
horse.

Hackney Saddle
A riding saddle, as distinct from a pack-
saddle.

Hadges
Hogs.

Hair
1. Used in plastering walls and
ceilings.
2. *Hair Cloth.

Hair Cloth
A stiff, wiry cloth made of horse hair
(taken from the mane and tail) and
perhaps linen or cotton, which might
have a variety of uses; e.g. the mat on
which *malt was spread to dry over a
kiln, a sieve, the side of a *keep (to
allow ventilation), etc.

Hair Line
Rope or line made of hair.

Hair Ranger
Sieve made of horse hair.

Hake
1. Hook over the fire, from which pots
hung.
2. *Heck.

Halberd, Halbert

A weapon: a cross between a battle-
axe and a spear, mounted on a handle
between 5 and 7 feet long.

Hale
Iron bar for hanging hooks. (Sfk)

Half Ewe
A half-grown ewe.

Half Hake
Small *harquebus or portable firearm.

Half Headed Bedstead
Bed with short corner posts, head-
board of medium height, and either
no *tester, or a canopy covering only
the head of the bed.

Half Pipe
Measuring vessel, usually of the same
capacity as a *hogshead.

Halfendeal
A half-share; a moiety.

Halfling
Half-grown, young animal. (Lin; Yks)

Hall, Hall House
The hall of a house; its main, or
perhaps its only room.

Hall Canvas
Canvas used to make *halling or
*hangings (2).

Halling
Tapestry, or stained/*painted cloth
used as wall *hangings (2).

Hallowmas
All Saints Day.

Hallyards
Lines for hoisting sails, flags, spars, etc.

Halme
1. A handle. (Oxf)
2. *Helm (2).

Halver
One who fishes with a *haaf net.

Hambargh
The collar of a draught horse.

Hambling
Lamed or docked. (Con)

Hamborough
1. A fine woollen cloth, originating in
Hamburg.
2. Timber imported from Hamburg.

Hames
The two curved pieces of wood, which
formed a horse's collar, with hooks to
which the traces were attached, so that
the horse's shoulder did the pulling.

Hammer Mandrel
Implement with a hammer on one side and an axe on the other.

Hamper
Large wicker basket with cover, used as a packing case for clothes.

Hanap
Drinking goblet, especially one used by the chief guest.

Hanch
Upright part of a gate to which hinges are attached. (Dev)

Hand
Linear measure.

Hand Board
Tray.

Hand Diaper
Hand towel of *diaper.

Hand Hook
A short iron book, with a wooden handle, used by tanners to move hides.

Hand Iron
*Andiron.

Hand Mill
*Quern.

Hand Screen
Hand-held 'screen', intended to shield the face from the heat of the fire.

Hand Spike
A sailor's tool; crowbar, usually of wood spiked with iron.

Hand Waiter
Elaborate serving tray.

Hand Wiper
Handkerchief (slang term).

Handkerchief Buttons
Worn by lovers on their hats: a miniature handkerchief decorated with tassels and fancy buttons.

Handle Bowl
Bowl with a long handle, used in brewing.

Handle Cratch, Handles, Pair of
A *cratch in which teazles were fixed to raise the nap on woollen cloth.

Handle Stock
Wooden handle.

Handler
Pit for 'handling' or soaking hides in a weak solution of tannin.

Hanger
1. Loop or strap on a *girdle, for attaching a scabbard to carry a sword, or for carrying keys.
2. *Hangings.
3. *Hangles.
4. A short sword.

Hanging Cupboard
A cupboard hung on the wall, rather than standing on its own, or perhaps a wardrobe for hanging clothes.

Hanging Glass
Glass mirror hung on the wall.

Hanging Lock
Padlock.

Hanging Press
A wardrobe in which clothes could be hung.

Hangings
1. Iron hooks attached to the chimney breast, from which cooking utensils were hung over the hearth.
2. *Painted cloth or tapestry hung on a wall or bedstead.

Hangles
Chains in a chimney from which pots and pans were hung on *pot crooks.

Hangrell
For hanging bridles, halters, etc., in a stable. (Ham)

Hanley Ware
Earthenware from Hanley Castle, Worcestershire.

Hannaborough, Hanyburrow
*Hambargh.

Hapharlot
A coarse bed covering or coverlet. (Bdf)

Happing
Rough cloth, bed-clothes, wraps. (Dur; Yks)

Happintree
Stumps in front of a waggon when the shafts have been pulled out; pole of a *coop (3). (Lin; Yks)

Haras
Mixed crop; perhaps peas, beans, and oats. (Nth)

Hard
1. When applied to livestock, barren.
2. *Hard Corn.

Hard Corn
Wheat or rye, as opposed to barley and oats.

Harden, Harne
Very coarse linen cloth made from
the *hurds of flax and hemp refuse;
cheaper than ordinary linen, used for
cheap sheets.

Harled
Speckled or mottled, applied to cattle.
(Yks)

Harmless
Free from loss or any liability.

Harness
1. The body armour of a soldier,
whether cavalryman or foot-soldier; a
suit of mail.
2. That part of a loom which shifts the
warp threads alternately to form the
shed.

Harness Press
For pressing clothes.

Harnessed
Mounted with silver or other metal.

Harnise, Hurns
The device in a loom that raises and
lowers the warp to form a shed. (Dev)

Harpsicord
A keyboard instrument; the strings
were plucked by quills rather than
being struck by hammers.

Harquebus
Short gun used by infantry; it had to
be supported by a tripod or rest when
being fired.

Harrateen
A linen fabric used for bed curtains.

Harrow
Heavy timber frame, set with *tends,
and dragged over ploughed land to
break up the clods or cover seeds once
they had been sown.

Harrow Buns
Cross-pieces of timber on a harrow,
into which its *tends are set.

Hartshorn
Products made from antlers: knife
handles, etc.; antlers could also be
used to produce a liquid from which
ammonia was obtained for smelling
salts.

Hassock
Clump of turf or matted vegetation,
especially of coarse grass or sedge.

Hastener, Haster

A stand or screen for concentrating the
heat of a fire on a joint of meat during
cooking.

Hasting
An early –ripening pea.

Hatch, Latch, and Catch
Lower half of a divided door, with its
fastenings.

Hatchell
Implement for hackling hemp, i.e. for
combing and sorting hemp fibres; see
also *Hackle.

Hatchet
1. A light axe with a short handle, for
use with one hand.
2. A small row or cock of cut grass.
(Oxf)
3. A mason's dressing hammer. (Oxf)

Hatchment
*Escutcheon; a square or lozenge-
shaped tablet exhibiting the heraldic
arms of a deceased person.

Hauberk
A coat of mail.

Haulm
*Helm (2).

Haulmere
*Aumbry.

Haver
Oats. (Dur; Yks)

Hawding
Stock pigs for breeding, not intended
for sale. (Lin)

Hawkey
A white-faced heifer or cow, or simply a
cow. (Yks)

Hawser
A large rope used for towing ships.

Hay Croke
Central remnant of a haystack. (Dby;
Ntt)

Hay Spade
A heart-shaped spade, with a sharp
edge, used to cut hay.

Head Cloth
1. A covering for the head.
2. Cloth hung over the head of a bed.

Head Piece
Head armour, helmet.

Head Tow
The loop on a plough to which the
`short-chain' or draft chain is attached.

(Con; Dev)

Headborough
A petty constable.

Headland
Strip of land where the plough-team turned at the end of the furrow.

Headstall, Headstand
That part of a bridle which fits around the horse's head.

Head Stock
The frame over a mine-shaft supporting the winding gear.

Healds
Small cords through which the warp passes in a loom.

Healing Stone
*Hilling Stone.

Heardes, Hewards
Bundles of *tow of a certain size. (Chs)

Hearse
Elaborate framework carrying lighted candles placed over the bier or coffin at funerals.

Hearying Barrel
Barrel used in malting. (War)

Heater
Metal box with wooden handles, heated by inserting hot metal strips, and used to keep smoothing irons warm.

Heck
Rack, usually for hay and other animal fodder; may also be used for cheese.

Heckall, Heckle
*Hackle.

Heder
Male lamb of eight to nine months, before its first shearing.

Hedgebote
The right to materials for maintainance of fencing.

Heifer
A young cow, from one year old until she bears her second calf.

Heirloom
Chattels left to the heir.

Helm
1. The haft of a hammer, spade or other tool; a handle.
2. Straw, especially when tied up in bundles ready for thatching.

3. A cattle-shed in the fields. (Northern)
4. A *belfry. (Lin)
5. A quantity of rye or oats.

Helm Balk
Loft for storing *helm (2).

Hemp
A plant of the cannabis family, from the fibres of which coarse fabrics and ropes were made.

Hemp Brake
An instrument for peeling the outer skin of hemp from its core.

Hemp Butt, Garth, Land
Field for growing *hemp, usually small.

Hemp Hards
The hard fibre of hemp or flax.

Hemp Line
String made from spun hemp.

Hemp Maul
Heavy hammer or *beetle, usually of wood, for beating the fibres of hemp.

Hemp Rack
Frame for stretching hemp.

Hemp Stock
Hemp drying frame.

Hempen
Medium coarse home-spun linen made from hemp.

Hempot
*Hamper. (Sal)

Hemptery
*Hempen.

Hengels
*Hangings .

Herbage
The right of pasturage.

Herd
The keeper of a flock or herd of domestic animals; a herdsman or frequently a shepherd. (Dur)

Herdes
*Hurds.

Hereditament
Property which descends to the heir under common law; any kind of property that can be inherited.

Heriot
The render due to the lord on the death of a tenant, usually the best beast, but cash payments might also be accepted.

Hesp
Hank of yarn, of a definite quantity.
Hewer Iron
Reaping hook.
Hewing Blade
Axe.
Hewke, Huke
Cape or cloak with a hood, worn by women, and subsequently by men. (Lin)
Hey
An enclosure.
Heyment
Ring hedge. (Chs)
Hiere Picra, Pigre
Purgative drug made from aloes and carella bark.
High Bedstead
*Standing bedstead.
High Day
Holy day; a festival day.
Hiller
A covering, a lid. (Ntt)
Hilling
1. Covering, usually of beds, but occasionally of tables.
2. A roof.
Hilling Stone
Stone or slates for roofing.
Hind
A servant or agricultural labourer.
Hinge Lock
Padlock.
Hip-shot
Having a dislocated hip.
Hitched Land
Part of the common field withdrawn from the customary rotation, especialy in the fallow year, and used for a particular crop such as vetches. (Bdf)
Hobbing Iron
1. Part of a grate or fireplace.
2. A shoemaker's tool.
Hobby
Pony or small horse.
Hock Monday
The second Monday after Easter, when money was collected for the church and parish before the Reformation.
Hod
Receptacle for carrying coal.
Hodge

*Hog.
Hog
1. A pig, especially a castrated boar, raised for slaughter.
2. A yearling sheep, not yet shorn.
Hog Colt
Young horse: a yearling foal.
Hog in Feeding
Pig being fattened for killing shortly.
Hoggerel
*Hog (2).
Hoggett
1. A sheep from weaning to its first shearing; a yearling sheep.
2. A two-year old boar.
3. A year-old colt.
Hogherd
A person who tends hogs.
Hogshead
Cask for beer and other liquids, usually holding 63 old wine gallons (equal to 52½ imperial gallons), as prescribed by statute in 1423. When used for liquids other than beer its capacity may vary.
Hogswash
The swill when a hogshead is washed out; it was fed to pigs.
Holdfast
1. A small safe that could be locked. (Dur)
2. A vice, clamp, bolt or other device to hold something fast.
Holding
Animals kept as stock for breeding, rather than for slaughter.
Holland
Fine linen fabric (although it was sometimes coarse and unbleached); linen and cotton cloth glazed with oil and starch, originally imported from Holland where the soil was particularly suited to the growth of flax from which a high quality linen could be produced.
Holland Clome
Glazed earthenware imported from the Low Countries.
Hollock
A Spanish red wine.
Hollow Lace
Braid lace used for edging.
Hollow Ware

Bowl or tube-shaped utensils of earthenware, wood, or metal.

Holmes
*Fustian made at Ulm, Germany.

Holster Cap
Leather pistol case worn on the belt, or fixed to the pommel of a saddle.

Holt
Plot where osiers or willows are grown.

Homper
1. Hammer. (Oxf)
2. Measure of six pecks. (Oxf)

Hone
Whetstone for sharpening knives, etc.

Hook
1. Usually s-shaped for hanging pots.
2. Sickle.

Hooker, Howker Bote
Fishing smack with one or two masts.

Hoop
1. A measure of corn of varying capacity.
2. A quart pot or tub bound with hoops. (War; Wor)
3. A finger ring.
4. *Hopper.

Hop Pitch
Iron crow-bar with a thick square point, used to make holes for hop poles. (Ess)

Hopper, Hoppit
1. A basket, especially the basket in which the sower carries his seed; a *seedlip.
2. A cheese vat.

Horn Book
*Battledore .

Horreum
Barn or storehouse (Latin).

Horse
1. Frame or stand on which to place barrels, vats, etc.
2. *Trestles .
3. Wooden framework for drying clothes.

Horse Corn
Beans and oats.

Horse Flesh
1. Reddish-brown coloured cloth.
2. Live horses (not dead ones!).

Horse Harrow
*Harrow pulled by a horse.

Horse Hilling
Covering for a horse.

Horse Lock
Hobble or shackle for a horse's foot, to prevent it straying or whilst it was being shod; it might be of iron with the owners mark on it to establish identity.

Horse Mill, Milne
Mill powered by a horse pulling a beam attached to gearing, and walking in a circle.

Horse Pistol
Large pistol carried at the pommel of a saddle on horseback.

Horse Pot
Round wooden vessel containing a quart or peck of grain.

Horse Rack
A manger holding fodder.

Horse Tree
Piece of wood to which the *swingletree of a harrow is attached.

Hose
Breeches and stockings treated as a single garment, covering loins and legs, sometimes also covering the foot like a long stocking, and worn with a *doublet.

Hostry
1. An inn or lodging room.
2. An ostler's room.

Hotes
Oats.

House
1. The whole house.
2. Room set aside for a specified purpose, e.g. the malt house, which may be inside the house, or an outbuilding.
3. The *hall.

House Coarsing
Brick laying.

House Sward
Land for a house.

Household Stuff
Miscellenous items of household furniture and/or utensils.

Housewife Cloth
Middling grade of cloth for various uses.

Housing Cloth
Sheet placed on a horse's back under

the saddle, or over the goods carried on its back.

Hovel

1. Storage shed or outhouse, usually without sides (although in Essex one was `over the buttery'). Used to store farm implements and produce, or perhaps for cattle and other animals.
2. The frame or stand on which a rick of corn is built, or on which peas or hay can be dried, perhaps with a thatched cover.

Howre Leder

Over leather, used for boot and shoe uppers. (Dby)

Hoy

A small coastal vessel, used in carrying passengers and goods for short distances.

Hub

1. *Nave.
2. The hilt of a sword or dagger.
3. A small amount of hay. (Oxf)

Huckaback, Huggaback

Strong linen fabric with a roughened surface, used for towelling.

Huckmuck

A wicker strainer placed in the bottom of the *mashing fat to strain new beer.

Huckster

Pedlar, hawker, or small shop-keeper.

Huke

Cloak or cape with a hood, worn as an outer garment.

Hull Bed

Mattress filled with wheat hulls or husks.

Humber

Grayling: a freshwater fish.

Hungry Hide

A hide in the process of tanning.

Hurden

*Harden.

Hurds

The coarser part of flax or hemp, separated with a *hatchel.

Hurl

Hurdle. (Dev)

Hurle Bed

A Scottish term for a *truckle bed.

Hurst Staff

Wooden staff.

Husbandman

Smallholder; one who tills the land.

Hustlements

Household goods and chattels of little value, not worth separate mention.

Hutch

1. Small, lightly built boarded chest, box, coffer, or cupboard, on legs (or perhaps hung on a wall), used for the storage of corn, meal, etc.
2. A trough.

Hyssop

Aromatic herb used medicinally.

Ile

Side aisle in a room, perhaps separated by a screen.

Ilte

*Gilt.

Imagery

Embroidered, painted or carved figures or decorations.

Impell

*Implements

Implements

A collective noun applied to things such as household furniture, stores, or utensils; may include animals.

Imprimis

In the first place (Latin).

Impropriate

Held by a lay owner (referring to tithes or ecclesiastical property).

In Stuff

Things belonging to the household, rather than to the farm.

Indenture

Deed between two parties, written out twice on the same sheet of paper or parchment, and cut along an indented or wavy line, so that each party had a copy. Its authenticity could be judged by matching up both copies.

Inderkin

Coarse German fabric made from poor hemp, used for towelling.

India Back Chair

Chair with a high hooped back, carved with Indian ornamentation; the design probably originated in Holland.

Indigo

A blue vegetable dye, originally from

India.

Indument
An ecclesiastical garment, robe or vesture.

Infield Land
Land close to the farmstead, which is regularly cropped; arable land.

Ink Horn
Ink pot, originally made of horn.

Inkle
Coarse linen tape or braid, or the yarn from which it is made, much used for shoe-laces, girdles, garters, apron strings, etc.

Innholder
Innkeeper.

Inning
Harvesting; hence `inned', harvested.

Inset Work
Marquetry.

Intake
A temporary enclosure, often taken illegally from the waste. (Northern)

Issue
Offspring.

Iorney
*Journey.

Ioynt
*Joint.

Ireware
*Iron Stuff.

Iris Root
Root of the Iris florentina, used powdered as a perfume and in medicine.

Irish Cloth
A cloth of wool or linen.

Irish Mantle
A blanket or plaid made in Ireland.

Iron
1. Iron rack for holding tobacco pipes in the fire to burn out impurities of tar, nicotine and carbon.
2. An iron weapon; a sword.

Iron Back
Fire back, protecting the back of the hearth, and usually decorated.

Iron Bound Wheels
Wheels with an iron rim to reduce wear.

Iron Chimney
*Chimney.

Iron Goose
Tailor's smoothing iron.

Iron Lane
*Lane.

Iron Stuff, Ware
Various small implements and utensils made of iron.

Iron Team
The chains used to harness oxen and horses to ploughs or wains, etc.

Iron Tow
Chains or links for towing; see *tow (2).

Iron Traces
Harness of long chains worn by the lead horse in a team; see also *traces.

Ironing Box
Smoothing iron made of brass or steel with a wooden handle. It had a cavity to hold a heated piece of metal which formed the base of the iron.

Isinglass
Form of gelatine obtained from fresh water fish, especially the sturgeon, used in food preparation for making jellies; also in the manufacture of glue, and for other purposes.

Italian Iron
Cylindrical iron with a hollow for the heater, used for fluting or crimping lace, etc.

Jack
1. A mechanical device for turning a spit; either driven by weights, or actuated by the draught of hot air rising in the chimney (a *smoke-jack); anything else that has a mechanical motion.
2. A short, close-fitting leather *doublet, stuffed with *tow, and sometimes plated with iron fastened together with cords.
3. A large leather drinking vessel.
4. A handle.
5. A device for lifting heavy weights.
6. A privy.

Jack Back
Strainer used to strain the *wort from the hops.

Jack Leg
Clasp knife; a pocket knife.

Jack Pot
A leather tankard or drinking vessel.

Jack Towel
Towel on a roller.

Jacobus
Gold coins struck in the reign of James I, worth 20s originally, but more later.

Jaconet
Type of muslin, originally from India.

Jade
A horse of inferior breed; one that is in poor condition or is worn-out.

Jag
Measure of the amount of hay that could be carried by a pack horse or on a cart.

Jagger
A carrier, carter, pedlar or hawker; one who carries goods by pack horse, and especially (in Derbyshire) lead ore.

Jagging Iron
Staff with a prong for lifting root vegetables.

Jake
*Close Barrell or stool; a privy.

Japanned
Treated with a black resinous varnish or lacquer which hardens and dries when heated. An oriental style, but not necessarily imported.

Japan Glass
Lacquered glass with Japanese ornamentation.

Jasper
A precious stone, often green.

Javelin
A pike or lance: a pointed weapon with a long shaft for thrusting.

Jean
Twilled cotton cloth, originally a type of *fustian, from Genoa.

Jell
*Deal, plank.

Jemmel
Hinge consisting of an eye and a hook.

Jennet
Carpenter's adze.

Jer Gear
Pieces of iron.

Jerkin
A short coat or jacket, often made of leather or frieze, worn by men.

Jersey
1. Fine knitted wool; worsted made from finest wool.
2. Worsted wool, combed and ready for spinning.

Jersey Wheel
Spinning wheel for making *jersey, used for stockings, etc.

Jestern
A light coat of mail, consisting of iron plates riveted to each other, or to some stout lining material.

Jet
1. Large ladle used in brewing.
2. Lignite: a coal-like substance which can be carved and polished, making jewellery.

Jib
*Gib

Joicing
*Agistment

Joined, Joint, Joyned
Beds, stools, and other furniture made by a joiner using mortice and tenon joints, fixed with pegs and dowels, rather than with nails; furniture with legs turned on a lathe.

Jointer
A long plane used to dress the edges of boards for jointing.

Jointure
Property granted to a wife for life, the grant taking effect on the death of her husband.

Joists
*Agistment.

Journey
One load; the amount of corn etc. carried in one journey.

Joyces
Joists: the cross pieces of timber comprising the framework to support a floor.

Julep
Sweetened drink used medicinally.

Jump Coat
A coat reaching to the thighs, open or buttoned at the front, with long sleeves, divided at the back to the waist. (Dby; Sts)

Justment Grounds
*Agistment.

Kanstyke
Candlestick.
Kart Ladder
*Ladder.
Keams
A hair sieve. (Bkm)
Kedger
A small anchor or grapnel.
Kee
*Kine.
Keech
Cake of consolidated animal fat, to be made into candles by the *chandler (2).
Keele, Keeler
1. A *cooler; a shallow tub for cooling milk or wort.
2. A small shallow vessel, operated by two or three men, used for transporting goods to and from sea-going ships. (Dur)
Keep
1. Storage cupboard for food, sometimes made of glass, usually with perforated bars or sides of *hair-cloth to allow air circulation.
2. The stop in a door frame.
Keeper
1. Sick nurse.
2. Device for keeping a clasp in place.
3. Fire dog or *andiron.
Keeve
*Keive.
Keive
Vat or barrel used in brewing, for washing clothes and bleaching, and for a variety of other purposes.
Keever
1. A shallow wooden tub into which cider was racked, or for cooling the *wort in the process of brewing.
2. Cover for a dish.
Keever Cart
A tipping cart. (Chs)
Keeving
Racking process in making cider. (Chs)
Kell Decking
A wooden platform for standing a *keele.
Kelter
Coarse cloth used for outer garments.

Kench
1. Strip of land in an arable field, containing a number of furrows.
2. A measure of wheat. (War)
Kendal
Green woollen cloth from Kendal, Westmorland.
Kenten
Fine linen cloth, originally made in Ghent.
Kercher, Kerchief
A woman's head cloth; a handkerchief.
Kerf
Notch made by a saw
Kern
A churn. (Dur)
Kersey
Coarse narrow and ribbed woollen cloth, woven from long wool; shorter and narrower than *broad cloth. Originally from Kersey in Suffolk.
Ketch
A sea-going vessel with two masts.
Kettle
Open cooking pot with semi-circular handles on both sides to suspend it over the fire; sometimes covered and used for boiling water.
Kettle Pan
Four-handled pan.
Kib
1. Tub for drawing water from a well. (Dby)
2. Thick, narrow spade for use in stony or hilly ground where a plough cannot be used.
Kid
A bundle of faggots used for firewood, or perhaps to be embedded in a bank, beach, etc., to give firmness to the ground.
Kidderminster Stuff
*Carpets and wall hangings of *Linsey Woolsey material manufactured in Kidderminster, showing a pattern formed by the intersection of two differently coloured threads.
Kilderkin
Cask to hold 18 gallons of beer or 16 gallons of ale, in accordance with a statute of 1531/2; other commodities, e.g. butter, might also be stored in

kilderkins of various sizes.

Kill

1. Kitchen.
2. *Kiln.

Kiln

Oven or drying frame, usually for *malt or hops. The *malt was laid to dry on a *hair cloth, well above the fire which was of burning straw. Other types of fuel made too much smoke and tainted the *malt. Also used for baking, burning lime, etc.

Kiln Hair

*Hair cloth used for drying *malt.

Kiln House

Room or out-house for baking, or for drying grain, especially *malt for brewing.

Kilp

1. Iron hook in the chimney from which pots are suspended.
2. Detachable pot handle.

Kilter

*Furniture. (Ess)

Kimblin

*Kimnel.

Kimnel

1. Cask or tub made of upright staves hooped together, made by a cooper, and used for brewing, baking, salting bacon, etc.
2. A shallow wooden vessel for milk to set in.

Kinderkin

*Kilderkin.

Kine

Cows, usually the milking cows in a herd.

Kine Vat

Cattle trough.

King's Beam

Official scales for weighing tin. (Con)

King's Iron

Large wedge.

Kinsman

A relative by blood or marriage, usually outside of the immediate family.

Kip

1. *Kipskins.
2. *Kipe.

Kipe

Bushel basket, made of osier with twisted handles on either side at the top, broad at the base, narrowing towards the top, with a capacity of 70 lbs, usually for fish.

Kipskins

Hides from large calves or small breeds of cattle, from which was derived a supple leather suitable for coat and shoe uppers, etc.

Kirn

Churn. (Dur; Yks)

Kirtle

1. Woman's outer petticoat, short skirt, or gown.
2. A man's coat or tunic, reaching at least to the knees.

Kit

Any hooped and staved wooden vessel with a handle or handles (perhaps fashioned from one of the staves), and sometimes a lid; used for holding or carrying milk, butter, fish, etc. or perhaps as a milking pail.

Kiver

A shallow wooden vessel or tub.

Kiving Vat

Large wooden tub used in brewing or in the dairy.

Knack Tub

Tub in which bread is kneaded. (Dur)

Knead Cowl

*Dough Cowl.

Knead Turnell

A shallow oval tub or trough in which curds were kneaded to squeeze out the whey; or in which dough was kneaded.

Kneading Trough

Wooden trough or tub on legs for kneading dough; it had splayed sides, and a partition down the middle, so that it could hold dough and flour.

Knechyn

*Knitch.

Knee, Knie

1. Piece of naturally bent wood useful in waggon construction.
2. A large angle bracket.

Knell

The church bells' slow chime when being rung for a funeral.

Knight Service

Feudal form of land tenure in

exchange for military service.

Knit Hose
Hose that has been knitted.

Knitch, Knitchin
A bundle of flax or hemp.

Knitting Table
Table used in knitting.

Knop
Ornamental knob, particularly on the end of a spoon.

Knot
A quantity of yarn or thread.

Kye
*Kine.

Lace Loop
Lace with patterns of small net worked in.

Ladder
1. Framework added to the sides or back of a *wain to hold in large loads of hay, etc.
2. Frame in the form of a ladder for storing cheese.

Lading
Made of lead.

Lading Piggin
A *piggin adapted for baling out water from boats, etc.

Lags
The dregs remaining in a cask, etc., when the liquor has been drawn off.

Laid
Trimmed, embroidered.

Lair
Cowshed or shelter for livestock.

Lair Stone, Layerston
Gravestone. (Northern)

Lamballe
Fabric made in Lamballe, Brittany.

Lamb Tow
Lambs' wool when shorn.

Lammer
Amber.

Lampblack
The carbon or soot made by burning oil lamps

Land
*Selion or strip of arable in the open field; about half an acre.

Landirons
*Andirons, or a type of grate if in the singular.

Lane
Iron ring at the end of a plough to which the horse is yoked. (Lin; Yks)

Langsettle, Long Saddle
A long wooden seat with high back and ends; a *settle . (Yks; Lin)

Lanneret
Male lanner falcon.

Lanon
*Andiron.

Lantern, Lanthorn
From the Latin, Lanterna. A portable light, which might be carried on a stave, with metal walls and panels of horn, protecting a candle flame.

Lapis Lazuli
A silicate containing sulphur, giving a bright blue pigment.

Lapis Tutty
Tutty: crude oxide of zinc, or calamine, used medicinally in a stringent ointment or lotion.

Lap
1. To cover.
2. To cut and polish cutlery.
3. Leaf of a table.
4. The end of a piece of cloth.

Lap Table
Small board placed on the lap as a substitute for a table.

Larder
Storage room for meat and other provisions.

Larking Bell
Device to attract larks into a net. (Wor)

Larnder
A wooden trough. (Dev)

Last
1. Wooden model of feet on which shoes and boots are shaped or repaired.
2. A commercial measure of weight, quantity or capacity.

Latch Pan
Pan placed under meat being cooked to catch the dripping. (Sfk)

Lath
Strip of wood used to form a wall or partition, and in building work; also used as a framework for slates and tiles.

Lathe

A barn or cow-house. (Northern)

Lather, Lether
Ladder.

Lathing Iron
An iron cross used to hold cross *laths whilst they were being nailed to long *laths.

Latt
*Lath.

Latten
A yellow alloy of copper, zinc, lead and tin, similar to brass, but weaker; used for cooking pots, candlesticks, etc. Often hammered into thin sheets.

Lattice
Structure made of *laths, used as a screen in windows without glass.

Latting Axe
Axe for splitting wood for *laths.

Laund Iron
1. *Andiron.
2. Smoothing iron for laundering.

Lavatory
Ritual washing of a priest's hands at the offertory, and after cleaning the communion vessels.

Laver
A metal wash basin or jug; a cistern, trough or conduit.

Lawn
Fine linen, resembling *cambric.

Lay
1. Type of pewter.
2. A local tax or rate.
3. *Lea.

Lay Metal
*Ley (2).

Layer
Piece of wood used in laying a hedge.

Layer Net
Net for catching game. (Dev)

Laystall, Laystow
Burial place.

Lazar
A leper or person with similar illness.

Lazy Back
A rod with serrated edges used to tip a *kettle without taking it off the *pot crook.

Lea
1. Measure of yarn.
2. Open land, usually grassland or pasture.

Lead
1. A large *cauldron, pot or kettle, not necessarily of lead (although it might be lined with lead), used in brewing or for various other purposes.
2. A *cistern .
3. A shallow lead tray used in separating milk.
4. Pigments, giving red and white colours.

Leading Strings
Reins to help children learn to walk.

Leaf
Very thin sheet of metal, especially silver or gold.

Leap
1. *Seedlip.
2. Half a bushel.

Leap Cloth
Cloth for a basket, especially a *seedlip.

Learning
Schooling.

Lease
Contract between a lord and a tenant, whereby the former grants land to the latter for a specified term in return for rent, usually an *entry fine, and perhaps a *heriot, etc. Also termed `*chattel lease', as they were *chattels which could be bequeathed by will, in contrast to freehold land, which could not.
2. *Leasow.

Lease and Release
A method of conveying freehold property.

Lease for Lives
A *lease granted for either 99 years, or for the lives of three named individuals, whichever is the shorter term.

Leases
Thread for sewing shoes. (Sry)

Leasow, Leaze
Pasture or meadow, which might be enclosed or common.

Leather Bark
Oak bark used in tanning leather.

Leather Bottle
Bottles made of leather, and coated

with tar or pitch, for carrying beer or cider to the fields at harvest time.

Leather Jack
Container for fluids; a *jack (3).

Leaven
Yeast, added to dough to produce fermentation.

Leaven Tub
Tub in which dough is fermented.

Leery
Empty. (South West)

Legg Wood
Logs cut from trees for use as firewood.

Lent Corn, Grain, Seed, Tilling
Any spring crop, usually barley or oats.

Letch
Vessel holding ashes for making *lye. (Dby)

Letching Knife
Knife for cutting meat into strips known as `letches'. (Wor)

Lettice
Whitish-grey fur, resembling ermine.

Lettice Bonnet
Bonnet made of *lettice, raised in a triangular shape over the head.

Leurey
*Livery.

Lever Tourn
Handle.

Ley
1. *Lea .
2. Alloy of tin and lead similar to *pewter. (Wor)
3. *Lay (2).

Ley Sword
The beating up apparatus in a *loom. (Dev)

Lid
Window shutter.

Lidging
Steeping ashes in water to produce *lye.

Life in Possession
The `life' named in a *lease currently occupying the property leased.

Lighter
Flat-bottomed barge, used for unloading (lightening) ships that are unable to reach a wharf, and for transporting goods by water for short distances.

Lights for Hot Beds
Glass cloches for the garden.

Lignum Vitae
The hard brownish green wood of the Guiacum tree, native to the West Indies; the resin from it, used medicinally.

Limbeck
Copper or glass apparatus used in distilling; a still.

Limber
Shaft of a cart, *wain, or carriage.

Lime Coop
Cart made close boards to carry anything which would fall through open boarding.

Lime Pit
Pit in which tanners dress skins with lime in order to remove hair.

Lime Weights
The weights to tension the warp in a vertical loom at which the weaver stood. (Dev)

Linch Pins
The pins which passed through the end of an *axletree to keep the wheels in place.

Line
1. The laced cord on the frame of a bedstead which supports the *bed, i.e. the mattress.
2. Flax or flaxen thread; the longer and finer fibres of flax or hemp. Hence `linen'.

Line, Linen Wheel
Small spinning wheel for flax.

Linen
Cloth woven from flax.

Ling
Species of salt-water fish, often dried or salted.

Linhay, Linney
Lean-to barn, perhaps with two storeys; the lower for animals and open to the weather, the upper for storage of hay, etc. (Dev)

Link(s)
1. Torch made of *tow and pitch, carried in the street at night.
2. Chains for hanging a pot over the fire.
3. *Fetters.

Linsey Wolsey
Inferior, loosely woven, coarse cloth made from a mixture of wool and flax, originally from Lindsey, Suffolk, and used for clothing or furniture by the poor.

Lint
Flax ready for spinning.

Lintel
1. The horizontal piece of wood or stone at the top of a door frame.
2. Tares in corn. (Dby)

List, Listing
The selvage, border or edge of a cloth, usually of different material from the cloth itself.

Litharge
Protoxide of lead, used as a pigment.

Lithe
Soft; sometimes used to describe *Grograin

Litster
A dyer.

Litten
A churchyard. (Ham)

Litting Tub
A dyer's vat.

Livery
A provision of food and drink, perhaps with lighting, taken to the *chamber at night.

Livery Cloak, Coat
Cloak provided by a lord to his retainers, and marked by his emblem so that their allegiance might be recognised.

Livery Cupboard
Small food storage cupboard, with a perforated door for ventilation, originally intended for the *livery, and kept in the *chamber. Sometimes it was hung on the wall; alternatively it might have legs. There might be a shelf with a canopy above the cupboard.

Livery Table
Table on which *livery, i.e. rations, were placed, or on which a *livery cupboard stood; a side table.

Lives
Term for which a *lease lasted, i.e. until the deaths of the `lives' named in the *lease.

Load
The specific quantity of particular commodities which customarily makes one load, e.g. 36 trusses of hay weighing 18 cwt; 40 bushels of wheat, etc.

Load Cart
Carts with detachable bodies and two wheels, drawn by a single horse. (Ess)

Load Horse
Pack horse. (Dby)

Lock
A quantity of wool hanging together; the short wool or fragments from a fleece.

Lock Saw
A long, tapering saw, used to make a place in the door for a lock.

Locker
Small cupboard with a lock for keeping valuables; sometimes built into a wall, or within a larger cupboard.

Locker Board
Table with a drawer or small cupboard beneath.

Lockeram, Lockram
Coarse loosely woven linen, originally from Locranon in Brittany, used for making shirts, etc., by the poorer classes.

Lodging Bed
Bed for an inn's guests, or for living in servants or lodgers.

Logger, Logget+
Log or block of wood fastened to a horse's feet to prevent it straying. (Oxf; War)

Logwood
The heartwood of an American tree used to make a black or dark-brown dye; also used medicinally. So-called because it was imported in the form of logs.

Longart
Tail or end board of a cart or waggon.

Longbow
The traditional English weapon - a six foot bow stave, with arrows three feet long that could be fired at the rate of six per minute.

Long Pepper

Condiment made from the immature fruit spikes of various peppers.

Long Wheel
Spinning wheel for wool. (Sal; Sts)

Long Saddle
*Langsettle

Loo Table
Round table designed to play a card game called loo.

Loom
1. An open vessel such as a bucket, tub, vat, etc., perhaps for use in brewing.
2. Machine for weaving yarn or thread into fabric by crossing threads known respectively as the warp and the weft.
3. An implement, tool, or utensil of any kind.

Loom Work
Woven material; weaving.

Loop
A jewel. (Con)

Loop Lace
Patterns of lace worked with a needle on a ground of fine net.

Lop Wood
Small branches and twigs lopped from a tree.

Lorimer
Maker of small iron ware, especially for use on a horse's bridle; a spurrier.

Lorry
A flat waggon on four low wheels.

Losset
A large flat wooden dish or tray, similar to a *voider .

Lount
*Selion or strip of land, separated from other lounts by a ridge. (Chs)

Love
Thin silk stuff much used for mourning clothes.

Low Bed
*Truckle Bed.

Lowse Crook
Implement for unyoking horses. (Dur)

Lozenge Board, Knife
Used for making diamond-shaped tablets for medicinal purposes.

Luce
A pike, i.e. the fish.

Lug

1. Long stick or pole; the branch of a tree.
2. Pole used in thatching.

Lumber, Lumberstuf
Odds and ends; disused objects; superfluous furniture.

Lustre
Glass chandelier.

Lutestring
Glossy silk fabric, in which the lustre and crispness is produced by heating and stretching the warp.

Lye
An alkaline solution used as an alternative to soap. Wood ash was placed in a tub with a perforated bottom, and soaked in water to wash out the soluble potash salts. Straw was steeped in the resultant solution; it was then slowly dried and burnt. The ash was rich in potash, and softened hard water on wash day.

Lymes
The place where skins were steeped in lime and water to whiten them.

Lysten
A coarse cloth or yarn. (Dev)

Mace
1. Spice made from the dried outer covering of nutmeg.
2. A knobbed mallet used to make leather supple.

Madder
A herbaceous climbing plant with yellow flowers, which produces a red dye.

Made Ware
1. Garments ready made.
2. Ware made up of different materials.

Maid
Applied to various inanimate objects, e.g. a clothes horse, a *trivet.

Maidenhair
Various different species of fern, much used in medicine.

Mail, Mail Coat
Armour made of chains or over-lapping plates.

Mail Pillion, Male Pillion
1. Saddle of *mail.

2. Leather or wooden saddle placed behind the rider for carrying a *male , i.e. luggage

Male
1. Travelling bag, wallet or pouch.
2. Heavy wooden hammer.

Maling Cords
Ropes for a pack saddle.

Malison
A curse or malediction.

Mall
*Maul.

Malligo
Raisins from Malaga.

Malt
Barley which has been steeped, germinated, and dried, for use in brewing.

Malt Mill
Mill for grinding *malt before brewing.

Malvesey
Malmsey: strong sweet white wine from the Mediterranean.

Manackles
Gauntlet.

Manchester Wares
Cotton goods made in Manchester.

Manchet
Fine wheaten bread.

Mandelion
A loose coat, sometimes sleeveless, worn by servants and soldiers as an overcoat.

Mandrel
1. Pickaxe, sometimes used in mining, with sharp points at each end.
2. Cylindrical rod around which metal is cast or shaped.

Manger
The trough, box, or rack in a stable or cow shed, from which beasts eat their fodder.

Mangle
A device for rolling and pressing cotton and linen clothing, etc., after washing.

Mankeing
Rake for clearing ashes in a bread oven. (Gls)

Manna
Juice from the bark of the manna ash, used as a gentle laxative.

Mantel, Manteltree
The piece of timber or stone above the front of the fire place, at the base of the flue; often having a shelf or mantelpiece.

Mantle
1. A loose, sleeveless cloak or overcoat.
2. Blanket of woollen cloth.
3. *Mantel.

Mantua
Loose fitting gown worn by women.

Map, Mappe
Tablecloth, napkins. (Dby; Dur)

Marble
Worsted cloth interwoven to resemble marble.

Marble Stone
Boulder found in glacial clay, used as a grindstone.

Mariner's Slops
Wide baggy breeches worn by sailors.

Mark
Unit of account, i.e. 13s. 4d. - but not an actual coin.

Marking Iron
Branding iron.

Marl, Marrell
Type of calcareous clay used as fertiliser.

Marline
Thin cord of two strands of thread.

Marmelet
Small *marmit.

Marmit
Large cooking pot, usually iron, fitted with hooks for hanging over the hearth.

Marrow
A companion, fellow-worker or partner. (Yks)

Marseilles Quilt
Patterned cotton fabric resembling quilting.

Marter
The fur of a marten.

Martinmas Beef
Beef killed and salted at Martinmas (November 1) ready for the winter.

Mase
*Mazer.

Mash Tub Horse
Stand for a *mashing fat.

Mashee
Papier mache. (Wor)
Mashing
Mixing *malt with warm water to make *wort, the first stage in brewing.
Mashing Fat, Keive, Stove, Tub, Vat
The vat in which the process of *mashing takes place.
Mashing Rule, Stick
For stirring the *malt in the *mashing fat.
Maskalyn
*Maslin.
Maslin
1. Mixed grain, especially rye mixed with wheat, used in bread-making; the bread made with this grain.
2. A metal alloy similar to brass; hence maslin ware.
Massard
*Mazer.
Massicot
Yellow protoxide of lead, used for pigmentation.
Mastic
A gum or resin exuded from the bark of various trees, and used medicinally.
Mat
Plaited rush or straw mat placed over the *cords of a bed, and under the mattress.
Match
1. Wick of a candle or lamp.
2. Three-yard long cord, soaked in pitch and tied around the waist of the musketeer, used to ignite gunpowder.
Mather
*Madder.
Matted Chair
Chair with a rush seat.
Matted Chamber
Room with matting on the floor.
Mattock
A type of pick-axe used for loosening hard ground, grubbing up trees, etc., one end of the blade was arched and flattened at right-angles to the handle, the other was spiked.
Mattress
Generally a *tick stuffed with flock, chaff, straw or hair.
Mattress Cords

*Cords.
Maul
A heavy hammer or club, perhaps used as a weapon.
Maund
1. Woven rush or wicker basket with handles and two lids, used for carrying eggs and butter to market.
2. A measure of weight or capacity.
Maundy
The ceremony of washing the feet of the poor, usually on Maundy Thursday in Easter week, by royalty or ecclesiastics, usually followed by the distribution of food, clothing or money.
May Butter
Unsalted butter, made in May to salve wounds.
Mazarine
A flat pierced plate, fitting into a larger dish, for straining water from boiled fish, etc.; a deep pie plate.
Mazer
A hard wood, used for making formal drinking cups or ornamental bowls; the cups themselves, which might also be made of maple or other hard wood, usually mounted on silver or gold; at a later date they might be made entirely of precious metals.
Meadow
Permanent grassland, primarily used for growing hay.
Meal
Ground grain; tub for storing it, or measure of it.
Meal House, Loft
*Boulting House.
Mealman
A dealer in *meal.
Mean Field
A field held in common, or in equal shares. (Chs; Lan)
Measuring Wheel
Device for measuring gunpowder for a fire-arm.
Meat
Food, diet - not necessarily meat.
Meat Board
Dining table.
Mechoacan

A Mexican plant whose tuberous roots were much used as a purgative.

Medley, Medley Cloth
Cloth woven from wool of various colours.

Mell
*Maul.

Mellay
*Medley.

Melting Kettle
Pot for melting solder.

Mercer
Dealer in textiles, etc.

Mercery
Collective term for the goods sold by a *mercer: fabrics of all kinds, as well as groceries.

Merchantry Ware
Trade stock; merchandise.

Mercury Precipitat & Sublimat
Quicksilver, used medicinally.

Mere
1. A boundary.
2. A measure of land containing lead ore. (Yks)

Mess of Pewter
Set of pewter dishes.

Messuage
Legal term for a dwelling house, with its outbuildings and land; originally, that portion of land intended to be or actually occupied by a dwelling house and its appurtenances.

Met
A measure of capacity. (Dby; Ntt)

Metheglin
Fermented liquor mad of honey and water.

Midden
Dung heap.

Milch
Milk.

Milch Kine
Milking *kine.

Milk Boy
Milk pail. (Dby)

Milk Churns
Container for making butter.

Milk House
Dairy.

Milk Spence
Milk can. (Yks)

Milk Trunk
Vessel into which milk was poured to be carried home from the field.

Mill
In probate inventories, usually a hand-mill or *quern for grinding *malt or mustard.

Mill Pick
Tool used for cutting grooves in, or corrugating, millstones.

Mill Puff
Type of *flock, used for stuffing mattresses. (Gls)

Millaine
Coarse fabric made in Milan.

Millions
1. Melons.
2. Mill irons, a tool for dressing millstones and giving them a rough surface.

Millwell
Cod fish.

Mind
Requiem mass in commemoration of a deceased person, on the anniversary of the funeral.

Mingled Stuff
Fabric woven from differently coloured threads.

Minikin
1. A plain weave worsted cloth, similar to baize.
2. A type of cotton.

Miniver
A type of fur used as lining and trimming.

Mithridate
A composition of various ingredients used as an antidote to poisons and infectious diseases.

Mitt
Tub or half barrel used for kneading dough, or for handling curds in cheese-making. (Sal)

Mittons
Gloves worn by a hedger to protect the hands from briars, etc.

Mixen
Place for storing manure; a dunghill.

Mizzen
Sail set on the mizzen mast.

Moarth

Lard or fat. (Con; Dev)

Moat, Mote
Cheese vat or mould.

Mob
Close-fitting cap with two lappets; a woman's night-cap.

Mockado
A fine cloth, originally made of mohair, but subsequently of either silk and wool, or silk and linen, with a pile surface. It originated in Flanders, and was made by Huguenot refugees in Norwich. Much used for clothing.

Mohair
Fine type of *camlet, closely woven, originally from the hair of angora goats, but later from silk or other fibres. It has a lustrous wavy pattern or finish.

Moiety
A half; one of two or more parts; a portion.

Mole Staff
Staff used to club moles.

Molette
Pair of pincers. (War)

Mona Dram
Chest and stand.

Mongcorn
*Maslin . (Gls)

Monks Chair
Table chair.

Monteith
Punch bowl with notches around its edge for suspending drinking glasses in water.

Months Mind
*Mind, held one month after death. Legacies to pay for the candles used in this service are often included in pre-reformation wills.

Moorstone
Granite used in the construction of *troughs, etc., as well as for house building. (Con)

Morde
*Moarth

Mordell
The share of her husband's property to which a widow was entitled.

Moreen
Woollen, or woollen and cotton, fabric,

imitative of mohair.

Moreles, Morlais
Cloth from Morlaix, France.

Morella, Morlay
A material used for dresses, curtains, etc.

Moringe Axe
Two-edged axe for rooting out stumps; a pick-axe. (Gls)

Morion
Steel helmet, without a visor or beaver.

Morocco
Goat leather, tanned with sumach, used in bookbinding and for fine upholstery.

Morris Pike
Type of pike, supposedly of Moorish origin; 16 or 18 feet long.

Mortar
Vessel used to hold ingredients whilst being pounded with a *pestle.

Morte
*Moarth.

Mortmain
Lands granted in perpetuity to an ecclesiastical body or other corporation.

Mortuary
Customary `gift' paid to the incumbent on the death of a parishioner, or to an ecclesiastical dignitary on the death of a priest within his jurisdiction.

Moryeve
Dowry. (Nth)

Moss Room
Rights on a `moss', i.e. an area of moorland, e.g. to take turves, sand, gravel etc., to pasture beasts. (Chs)

Mother Corn
Payment to the miller, by way of a proportion of the corn he has ground. (Dby)

Motley
Cloth of mixed colours. (Lan)

Mould
Loose or broken earth; surface soil.

Mould Rake
Rake in the plough.

Mould Screen
Cloche or garden frame.

Mould(ing) Board
1. A board or table for kneading

dough in bread-making.

2. The board or metal plate on a plough which turns over the furrow slice.

Moulds
Men's padded *drawers. (Ham)

Mourning Cap
Cap worn by a widow in mourning.

Mourning Gloves
Gloves to wear in mourning.

Mouse Snatch
Mousetrap.

Mourning Ring
A ring to be worn by a widow during the period of mourning for her husband.

Movables
Property such as furniture which could be moved, and is not fixed to the dwelling house.

Mow
A stack or rick of hay, corn, etc.

Mow Barton, Mowhay
Stack yard.

Mow Stack
*Rick Staddle.

Muck Crate
Wooden pannier for carrying manure to the fields on horse-back.

Muck Drag, Hack, Hook
Fork or implement with hooked tines for moving manure.

Mug
Drinking vessel with a handle but no lid.

Mullen
Bridle or head-gear for a cart-horse, with blinkers. (Oxf)

Mullet
1. Tweezers or pincers.
2. Grindstone or millstone for use by an apothecary or painter.

Mullock
Rubbish.

Multer
*Mother Corn.

Mum
A type of beer, originally brewed in Brunswick.

Muncorn
*Maslin.

Mung

Mixed food for horses: barley, oatmeal, bran, etc. (Northern)

Munger
Horse collar made of twisted straw.

Muntin
The central vertical piece of wood between two panels.

Murdering Piece
A wide bored hand gun which could be loaded with small pieces of metal to create a shrapnel effect when fired.

Murrey
Mulberry coloured, i.e. purple-red; cloth of this colour.

Murrian
*Morion.

Musketoon
A short musket with a large bore, used by infantry.

Muslin
Delicately woven cotton fabric.

Mustard Ball, Mill, Quern
Hand-mill or *quern for grinding mustard seed.

Musterdevillers
A mixed grey woollen cloth, originally produced in Montivilliers, Normandy.

Mydosalt, Mydsalt
A salt meadow or salt marsh, where sea-water is collected for the extraction of salt. (Lin)

Myrabalan
An astringent plum-like fruit, used for medical purposes.

Nadge, Nag
Small riding-horse or pony.

Nager
*Auger. (Lan)

Nail Bore, Passer, Percer
Gimlet or bradawl.

Nail
A measure of length for cloth, about 2¼ inches.

Nankeen
Crude blue and white, or richly enamelled, porcelain from Nanking in China.

Napery
Household, and, especially, table linen.

Napkin
1. A table napkin, essential when food

was eaten with the fingers.

2. A pocket handkerchief.

Napron
Apron.

Narke
Nail (Nth)

Nathe
*Nave.

Nave
Wheel hub, into which the *axle tree is inserted, and from which the spokes radiate.

Neap
The pole or shaft of a cart; the wooden rest for that shaft.

Neat
A cow, calf, ox, bullock, etc.; cattle.

Neckerchief, Neckinger, Neck Cloth, Neck Rail
*Kerchief worn around the neck.

Neeld, Nelde Work
Needle work.

Nest of Boxes
Chest of small drawers, as used by an apothecary.

Nether House
Low service room or outhouse.

Netherhead
Board at the rear of the cart which had to be let down when loading, or which could be extended to take an extra load. (Chs; Lan)

Netherstocks
Silk or woollen stockings worn below breeches or hose.

Nets and Engines
Devices for trapping birds, animals, vermin, etc.

New Sixpence
Coin with a milled edge, following the re-coinage of 1696, contrasted with *old money.

Nib
1. Grip on a scythe handle.
2. The shaft of a waggon.

Nigella Romana
Seed of Ranunculus, used medicinally.

Niggard
False bottom for a grate, reducing fuel consumption.

Night Cap
Skull cap with close upturned brim

worn in bed.

Night Stool
*Close barrel for use at night.

Night Table
Bed-side table.

Nimes Thread
Type of thread originally made in Nimes.

Nine
An indefinite period between a week and a fortnight. (Sal)

Nipper
Pincers, forceps or pliers.

Noble
*Angel.

Noddie
A light two-wheeled hackney carriage.

Nog
1. Small block of wood.
2. Handle of a scythe.

Noggen
Coarse fibres of flax or hemp; or rough linen made from it.

Noggin
Drinking cup, usually holding a quarter pint and made of earthenware; also refers to the quantity it holds.

Noil
Short pieces and knots of fibre combed out of wool; wool refuse.

Nonage
Under age, being a minor.

Normandy Canvas, Cloth
Canvas cloth from Normandy.

Notary Public
A person publicly authorised to draw up and witness legal documents, etc., a commissioner for oaths (commonly abbreviated `N.P.', i.e. notary public).

Notary Hole
Pigeon hole. (Gls)

Nowt
Cattle, oxen. (Yks)

Nuncuputive
Used of wills which were declared verbally, but not written until it was too late for the deceased to sign them.

Nun's Thread
A fine cotton thread, for sewing.

Nurse's Chair
Low chair used for nursing infants.

Nut

Cup made from, or resembling, a coconut shell, mounted on a metal foot.

Nut Coffer

*Coffer made of walnut.

Nycette

A breast cloth or light wrapper for the bosom and neck.

Nyld

Needle.

Oad

*Woad

Oakum

1. The coarse flax separated in hackling: *hurds or *tow .

2. Light fibres obtained by picking old rope, and used to caulk ships' seams

Oast Hair

Coarse open fabric made of horse hair, on which hops or malt were laid to dry over a kiln.

Ob

A half-penny.

Obit

A commemorative mass held on the anniversary of a persons death.

Oblation

Gift to the church.

Obligation

A legal agreement whereby a person becomes bound to another for the payment of a sum of money or performance of some service.

Occamy

An alloy resembling silver, perhaps made of copper, tin and zinc. The word is a corruption of `alchemy'.

Occupation

Use.

Offal Iron

Iron odds and ends.

Offal Wood

Waste wood: the trimmings of trees that have been felled; small pieces of wood for kindling.

Oge

A young sheep, not yet shorn. (Dur)

Ogee

A doubly curved moulding, convex above, concave beneath.

Oggyes

Highly ductile iron used for making arrow heads.

Oil Cloth

Waterproofed table cloth.

Oil de Bay

Oil from the bay laurel.

Oil of Spike

Oil from lavendula spica, used in painting, and for veterinary purposes.

Old Money

Coins minted before the 1696 re-coinage. After that date coins had milled edges to prevent them being clipped by forgers. Old money remained legal tender until 1733.

Oleron

A coarse fabric perhaps originating in Oleron, France.

Olibanum

An aromatic gum resin used as a medicine; frankincense.

Olive Wood

Wood of the olive, used in ornamental woodwork as it could be highly polished.

Ombres

Large cupboard in a stable for horse tackle. (Chs)

Orase

*Arras.

Orcanet

A dye, obtained from alkanet.

Orchel

A red or violet dye obtained from certain lichen.

Ordinary

A variety of *kersey.

Orfray, Orphrey

Rich embroidery, often gold, especially on ecclesiastical vestments.

Oriel

Large windowed recess, often projecting from an upper storey.

Ormolu

Gold or gold leaf prepared for gilding.

Orpharion

A large instrument with six to nine strings, played with a plectrum, and similar to a lute.

Orris

Lace patterned with gold or silver; embroidery made with gold lace.

Orris Root
*Iris Root
Osmund
Iron of a superior quality, used for arrow-heads, fish-hooks, etc., originally imported from the Baltic.
Osnaburg
Coarse linen originally made in Osnabruck.
Osset
Woven material, probably of wool.
Ossy
A sweet wine from Alsace.
Ostrey
Hostelry: inn.
Otter Stave
Long pole used in hunting otters.
Ottoman
Cushioned seat for reclining, without back or sides.
Ouch
Ornamental buckle or brooch, used to hold clothing together, and/or worn as an ornament.
Out Shot
Out-building or lean-to. (Northern)
Outing Vat
*Uting Vat.
Outnal
Brown flaxen thread from Oudenarde.
Over Leather
For making shoe uppers.
Overbody
Garment worn over bodice.
Overen
1. The top framework of a waggon. (Dur)
2. Odds and ends, remnants.
Overland
1. Land without a dwelling house. (Dev)
2. Land on the margins of commons or demesne land, that did not belong to a particular tenement, and that had no common rights attached to it. (Dev)
Overlay
1. Coverlet or cloak, cravat or neckcloth.
2. Harness for a pack horse. (Chs)
Overplus
Surplus; that amount which remains over from the main amount.

Overseer
Person appointed to supervise the carrying out of the terms of a will. Overseers of the poor are rarely mentioned in probate records.
Overthwart Saw
Cross-cut saw.
Ower Slag
Refuse of lead ore. (Dby)
Owl
A covered cup in the shape of an owl.
Owler Wood
Alder wood. (Northern)
Ox, Oxen
Any bovine animal, but particularly a castrated bull used as a plough-beast or for haulage purposes.
Ox Bow
U-shaped rod usually made of ash, which passed under the ox's throat and up through two holes in the yoke above, to hold the yoke in place.
Ox Drag
*Drag drawn by oxen.
Ox Rack
Manger for oxen.
Ox Stall
Stable for oxen.
Ox Teams
Equipment used to harness oxen to a plough, harrow, or cart.
Oxgang
Measure of land, c.10-20 acres varying by locality; an eighth of a carucate or ploughland.
Oyster Table
Table with a water-resistant top such as slate or metal, used for the preparation and eating of oysters.
Ozen
A coarse linen cloth, originally from Osnabruck, used for making rough hard-wearing clothing, or for furnishings, sacks, tents, etc.

Pack
A bundle of anything bound up together; a container for carrying goods on horse-back.
Pack Cloth
A cloth to wrap goods up for carriage, or to place under the *pack saddle.

Pack Saddle
Saddle with straps for carrying loads on the back of a pack horse.

Pack Saddle Tree
Rack for pack saddles.

Pack Thread
Twine or thread used for tying up packs or bundles.

Pad
1. A bundle of straw to sleep on.
2. *Panel .
3. A soft saddle or small cushion for a *pillion.

Padaway
A type of say or serge made in Padua.

Paddle
Small spade-like implement for cleaning a *plough share of earth and clods.

Paddle Staff, Stave
1. A long staff with an iron spike or small spade at its end, used by mole catchers, and also as a walking stick.
2. A spade-shaped implement used to mash the *wort in brewing.

Painted Border
A painted plaster frieze between the *wainscot and ceiling.

Painted Calico
*Calico with painted designs or pictures, in various colours.

Painted Cloth
Decorative wall hangings (to keep out draughts) or bed coverings, depicting religious scenes, mottoes, flower patterns, etc., painted in oils, and usually made of cloth or canvas. A cheap substitute for tapestry.

Painters Black
Black paint, dye, pigment or varnish.

Painters Oil
Linseed oil.

Painters Stone
Grinding stone for grinding up substances to make pigments.

Pair of Ruffs
*Ruffs worn on the wrist.

Pair of Stairs
A flight of steps, or a staircase with two landings.

Pair of Tables
The two folding leaves of a table on which games such as backgammon are played.

Paise
A weight, or a container to hold that weight.

Palaver
*Pillow bere.

Pale
Stake or strip of wood for fencing; often `pales and rails'.

Pall Cloth
Cloth to cover an altar or a coffin.

Pallet, Pallias
Straw-stuffed mattress; a mean or poor bed or couch.

Pampilion
A coarse woollen fabric with a rough surface.

Panade
A large knife.

Pancheon
1. A large, shallow, earthenware bowl, in which milk was allowed to stand in order to allow the cream to separate.
2. Cask with a quarter barrel capacity.

Paned
Strips of differently coloured cloth joined together.

Panel, Pannal
1. A piece of cloth placed under a saddle, or lining the saddle, to protect the horse's back from chaffing.
2. A wooden saddle for a donkey or ass; a crude form of saddle.
3. A pack saddle.
4. That part of *wainscot consisting of a thinner board set into the main framework.

Pannier(s)
1. Large light baskets (usually two) placed on either side of a horse's back, for carrying goods to market.
2. A saddle bag.

Pantofle
Footwear of various kinds, e.g., slippers, out-door overshoes.

Pap Pan
Pan used to keep food and drink warm.

Pap Spoon
Spoon for feeding infants semi-liquid or mashed food.

Paper Chamber

Room with *paper hangings.

Paper Hanging
Wall hanging, usually printed with ornamental designs; wallpaper.

Paper Window
Window with oiled paper in the place of glass.

Paragon
Rich double *camlet, used in upholstery; originally from the East.

Parcel
Piece or quantity of things, e.g. a piece of land of indefinite quantity, a small or moderate quantity of goods.

Parcel Gilt
Lightly or partly gilded silver, often having inner surface gilded.

Parell
*Apparel.

Parchment Lace
A type of lace, the core of which was parchment.

Paring Iron, Knyfe
Used for shaving skins in tanning, paring off edges, or for paring a horse's hooves.

Pariswork
A fine linen used for *napery.

Paritor
*Apparitor.

Parlour
Private sitting room used as a best room on special occasions, or as a best bedroom.

Parmacety
*Spermaceti.

Parse
A book of grammatical exercises.

Partizan
A pike with a long, double-edged blade, with various projections on each edge, which were mirror images of each other.

Partlet
Woman's neckerchief, collar or *ruff, perhaps to fit the low neckline of a dress, and perhaps of transparent gauze. Originally worn by both sexes.

Pash
Poker. (Northern)

Pashell
Pestle, *beetle, or mallet.

Passement
Gold or silver lace trimming.

Passer
A drill or gimlet, etc., for boring small holes.

Paste, Paste Board
Sheets of paper pasted together as a substitute for a board.

Pastern
Shackle attached to the foot of an animal, especially an unbroken horse, to prevent it from wandering.

Pastry
Room for storing food or utensils, or where pastry was made. (Bdf)

Patch Box
A box containing the small black patches which it was fashionable to apply to the face.

Pate
Skin from a calf's head.

Patel
Shallow pan or dish.

Paten
Shallow dish on which the bread used at the eucharist is placed.

Paternoster
A rosary, and especially that bead on a rosary which indicates that the Lord's prayer is to be said (from the Latin for `Our Father').

Patté
A cross on which the arms are almost triangular, meeting at the centre, and forming almost a square; similar to the Maltese Cross.

Patten
1. Flat wooden clog, raised off the ground by an iron ring which kept the wearer from sinking into the mud.
2. The foundation of a wall; a base plate or sill. (Hrt)

Patty Pan
Tin for baking small pies, tarts or pasties.

Pauncher
A belt or girdle. (Con)

Pavement
Could be used to refer to stone flags used as flooring inside a house, as well as to an outdoor path.

Pax

Tablet or board bearing a symbol of Christ, the Virgin Mary, or one of the saints, kissed by the priest and congregation before communion.

Pay of the Parish
Poor relief.

Pea Haulm
Used for thatching and litter.

Peas Hook
Hook for lifting pea haulms.

Peal, Peel
1. Paddle-shaped blade with a long handle, used for placing and removing bread, cakes, pasties etc. into and from the oven.
2. Pillow.

Pearling
Type of lace for trimming the edges of garments.

Pearling Cat
A utensil like a funnel used to coat *comfits with sugar.

Peason
Plural of pea.

Peat
Piece of turf cut for fuel.

Peck
1. Measure of capacity for dry goods: two gallons or a quarter of a bushel; a vessel able to hold that amount.
2. Raw skin of a sheep. (Sal)

Ped
A wicker pannier; a hamper with a lid, perhaps to carry mackerel. (Nfk)

Peel
1. A baker's shovel.
2. A fire shovel.

Peeling
Thin fabric or skin used as dress material.

Pell
*Pale.

Pelt
Undressed skin of a sheep or smaller animal.

Peltry
Rack or place where undressed hides were stored.

Pembroke Table
Small table on four legs with hinged flaps which could be raised to make it larger.

Pen
1. A movable chicken coop , perhaps kept in the kitchen. (Bdf)
2. A rack or shelf for storing dishes. (Bdf)

Penal Bill
Written *obligation to pay a fixed amount of money by a certain date, with legal penalty for non-compliance.

Pengjerd
*Porringer.

Penide
A stick of barley sugar, used as a remedy for colds.

Penistone
Coarse woollen cloth for garments, made in Penistone, Yorkshire.

Pennant
Sandstone from South Gloucestershire used as building material.

Penny
Small coin, worth one-twelfth of a shilling; made of silver until the reign of Charles II.

Pentis, Penthouse
A shed on the side of a house, especially one belonging to a smithy, where horses stood to be shod.

Pepper Corn, Powne, Quern
Hand-mill for grinding pepper.

Percer
1. Rapier or short sword. (Dur)
2. Any implement for piercing holes, e.g. an *auger, a gimlet.

Perch
1. A heavy stick used to beat cloth in the fulling process.
2. Wooden bars over which pieces of cloth were pulled to inspect or dress them.
3. Measure of length; one-fortieth of a *rood.

Performed
Fully set up, complete; e.g. a bed performed, a musket performed. (Con; Dev)

Perfuming Pan
Pan in which to burn incense, to fumigate, scent, or disinfect.

Perk
Wooden frame over which cloth was drawn so that it could be thoroughly

examined.

Perpetuana
Durable, glossy, wool fabric.

Perry
Drink made from pears.

Persian
Thin light silk for linings.

Perters
Appurtenances. (Gls)

Peruke
A wig, usually long.

Pestle and Mortar
A pounding implement and bowl.

Petronel
A large pistol or carbine often used by cavalry; the butt rested on the chest when firing.

Petticoat
1. A woman's skirt worn externally.
2. A man's small coat, worn beneath the *doublet; a waistcoat.

Pewter
A grey alloy of tin, lead, and sometimes other metals, used for dishes and plates, etc.

Pewter Frame
Shelves for displaying pewter.

Pewter Ring Stand
Metal circle on which a hot dish could be stood.

Phatt
1. Lead receptacle used for evaporating brine at Droitwich. (Wor)
2. *Vat.

Philemort
Feuillemort: a tawny colour.

Philip & Cheyney
Gloss woollen and silk cloth; kind of worsted stuff of common quality.

Philltugs
Two pieces of wood on a horse's collar, fastened by leather straps; chains were attached to each piece for the horse to pull its load.

Piano Nobile
The main storey, containing the principal reception rooms, of a gentleman's house.

Pick
Pointed, pronged or forked implement for fireside or agricultural use.

Pickell, Pike Evil

Pitchfork

Picking Hammer
Tiler's hammer. (Nfk)

Pie
Rules governing the occurrence of more than one `office' falling on the same day, for the use of clergy.

Pie Crook
Pie plate.

Piece
The weight or balance of a clock.

Pied
Parti-coloured: of two or more colours.

Pier Glass
Tall, narrow mirror, placed on the `pier' between two adjoining windows.

Pig Iron
A flat plate of iron hung on bars between the spit and the fire, when the latter is too hot.

Piggin
1. Small wooden milk-pail, with one stave longer than the rest to serve as a handle.
2. A wooden drinking vessel.

Pightle
Small field or enclosure; a close or croft.

Pig's Darn
A sow.

Pike
1. Pick or pitch-fork.
2. A very long staff with a spear on its head, carried by infantry (pikemen).
3. Temporary hay-stack in the fields, peaked to let the rain run off. (Dur)

Pike Stave, Stock
The shaft of a *pike (2).

Pilch
A light frameless saddle for children; a rug or pad laid on a saddle. (Midlands)

Pild, Pilled Hemp
Hemp from which the outer skin has been peeled.

Pill
To strip bark from trees for use in tanning.

Pillar and Claw Table
Table resting on a single pillar with a claw-shaped foot.

Pillion
1. Pad or small saddle attached to the

rear of the main saddle, for a second rider or a *male.

2. Light saddle for a female rider.

Pillow
Dish-shaped wooden block on which stone was placed for carving.

Pillow Bere, Cod
Pillow case.

Pillow Tie
Pillowcase. (Dor; Ham)

Pin
Small cask or keg holding 4.5 gallons. (Ssx)

Pin Block
Tool used by a currier; a wooden block set with pins on which leather was beaten to soften it.

Pin Bouk
Wooden bucket. (Dby)

Pin Wheel
Device used in linen weaving. (Chs)

Pingle
Small enclosure or paddock. (Dby)

Pinions
1. Short wool left in the comb after the long staple has been drawn off.
2. The skirt of a gown. (War)

Pink
Small sailing boat, flat-bottomed, with bulging sides, used for fishing and coasting.

Pinn
Small cask holding half a firkin of 4½ gallons. (Dby; War)

Pinner
1. Officer who impounds stray animals in the pinfold.
2. A cap or neck-cloth; a *coif with two long flaps.

Pinsons
Pincers.

Pint, Pinterpot
Pint pot or measure; a drinking vessel.

Pintado
Chintz: coloured cotton fabric often used for hangings or cloths.

Pipe
1. A large cask used for wine, and also for other liquids and provisions; its capacity was 126 gallons, 2 hogsheads, or half a tun.
2. Metal or wooden fitment on a

horse's collar, through which the reins pass.

Pipkin
Small earthenware (or, earlier, metal) pot or pan, round and deep, used in cooking.

Pirn
The spool or bobbin on which thread is wound for the weft.

Piss Pot
Chamber pot.

Pistol, Pistolet
A small fire-arm, held and fired by one hand.

Pistol Bottle
Bottle for carrying drink in one's pocket. (Hrt)

Pistolet
A Spanish gold coin

Pit Coal
Coal from a pit, as opposed to charcoal.

Pit Grate
Grating over a kitchen ash-pit.

Pitch
*Hop Pitch.

Pitch Brand
A distinctive mark of ownership on a sheep, made with pitch; the implement used to make the mark.

Pitch Skillet, Pan, Pot
Pan for boiling tar to make pitch when branding sheep, or on board ship.

Placard
Garment, often richly embroidered, worn beneath an open gown or coat.

Placebo
Vespers in the office of the dead, from the first word in the Latin service.

Plaid
Woollen cloth with a chequered pattern.

Plainer
1. Tool for smoothing sand or clay in a mould.
2. Tool for smoothing wood.

Plancherd, Planchin
Boarding made of wooden planks; a floor or ceiling so made.

Plane
1. The shaft of a crossbow. (Oxf)
2. A type of woollen cloth. (Chs)

Plank Table
Table top made of boards held together by battens, set up on trestles and taken down after use.

Plasher
Hedge layer.

Plaster
Curative substance spread on muslin and placed on the skin or wound.

Plat
Chart or plan.

Plate
Kitchen dishes of various kinds made from gold or silver.

Plate Coat
Leather corselet with small plates of iron sewn on.

Plate Ring
Table mat to protect the table from hot plates.

Plate Warmer
Plate with hollow bottoms for hot water, to keep it warm.

Plated
Furniture overlaid with metal plates for ornamentation or protection.

Platter
Flat dish of pewter, wood, or earthenware to hold food. Wooden platters were usually made of sycamore, they were always round, and thinner than trenchers.

Playing Table
Table for games such as chess, backgammon, and cards, perhaps with the appropriate markings.

Pleache
Hedging implement, designed to partly cut stems so that they could be bent down in order to make the hedge thicker; the cut stems would send up vertical shoots and thus renew the hedge.

Pleck
Small piece of ground, a plot, a small enclosure.

Pledge
Surety; anything handed over to another as security for performance of an agreement, etc.

Plitch
Thick hempen material. (Dev)

Plock
Blocks of sawn wood, sometimes also roots and stumps. (Gls)

Plough Beam
A long, curved timber or iron beam, the main part of a plough, to which all the principal parts are attached.

Plough Bote
Wood or timber which tenants could take from their tenanted property to make and repair ploughs and other implements.

Plough Chain
*Chain .

Plough Gear, Stuff
The harness, equipment and fittings of a plough.

Plough Irons
The *coulter, *plough share, and any other iron parts of a plough.

Plough Share
The pointed blade of a plough, which, following the *coulter, cuts the ground horizontally at the base of the furrow.

Plough Slip
Metal plate with two metal strips underneath, acting as a sledge to haul the plough from field to farmstead. (Dby)

Plough String
One of the traces of a plough.

Plough Timber
All parts of the plough which were made of wood.

Ploughwright
A person who makes ploughs.

Plow
Waggon. (Dor)

Plough Stilt
Handle of a plough. (Northern)

Ploughbote
The right to wood or timber for the construction and maintainance of a plough and other agricultural implements; a right normally enjoyed by tenants.

Plump
1. Pump.
2. Small, vertical butter churn. (Dor)
3. A cluster, bunch, or clump.

Plush
Rich cloth with a long nap used in

garments such as footmen's liveries, and in saddlery and upholstery.

Poatestone
Sharpening stone for tools. (Gls)

Pocket
A measure of hops; 1¼ hundredweight; sack or bag holding this amount.

Poddinger
*Porringer.

Point Maker
Maker of *points.

Point
1. Tagged lace or cord for lacing up clothes, e.g. attaching the *hose to a *doublet.
2. Needle.

Poite, Poyt
Poker. (Dby; Yks)

Poitrel
Breast plate for a horse.

Poke
1. A bag or small sack, especially one for carrying grain, etc., on a pack saddle.
2. A device to prevent animals breaking through fences. (Dur)

Poke Cloth
Sack cloth.

Poldavis
Coarse sacking or canvas frequently used for sail cloth; originally from Poldavide in Brittany.

Pole
1. Stake.
2. Long handle of a scythe.
3. Long pole used in dyeing.

Pole Axe
1. Battle axe with a long handle; a *halberd.
2. Butcher's axe for slaughtering, with a hammer on the opposite side to the blade.

Polke
Cupboard. (Dur)

Pollenger
Timber from pollarded trees, i.e. branches which have grown from stumps.

Pomade
A scented ointment or oil used as a perfume, or to dress the hair.

Pomander
Small receptacle or necklace containing an aromatic substance to scent the air and ward off infection.

Pomet Lace
Type of silk lace.

Pompillion
*Populeon.

Poniard
A dagger.

Poor Mens Box
Box for alms in the church.

Poppinjay
Fabric originally made in Poperinghe, in the Netherlands. (Wor)

Populeon
Ointment made from the buds of the black poplar.

Porket
A small or young pig.

Porr
A fire poker. (Dur)

Porringer
A bowl-shaped pewter or earthenware dish (or perhaps silver in wealthier households), often with a cover and ear-shaped handles, for porridge, soup, *potage, etc.

Portal
Partition or fixed screen within the door of a room to keep out draughts, made of *wainscot.

Portas, Porteous
A portable breviary or prayer.

Portmanteau
Trunk case or bag for storage of clothes or for carrying them when travelling.

Posnet
1. Small pot with a long handle and three short legs, used for boiling.
2. *Porringer.

Posset
Drink of hot milk curdled with ale, vinegar, or wine, perhaps mixed with spices or sugar, drunk as a delicacy or as a cure for colds.

Posted Bedstead
Bed with a canopy or *tester supported on four posts.

Posy
Verse or motto inscribed on a ring for the finger.

Pot
Round cooking vessel, deep rather than broad, and with three feet, to stand or hang over the fire.

Pot Brass
Alloy from which pots were made.

Pot Crooks, Gails, Hooks
*Crook.

Pot Hanger
*Hangings .

Pot Hangle
*Hangles

Pot Hooks
Hooks above a fire, from which pots could be suspended.

Pot Kilp
Movable hook or handle for hanging pots over the fire. (Northern)

Pot Links
The chain on which a *pot was suspended over the fire.

Pot Metal
Alloy of lead and copper used to make pots.

Potage
Thick soup, oatmeal, porridge, broth, etc.

Potash
Potassium carbonate, used in finishing woollen cloth, and for making soap.

Potgayle
Hook suspended from a bar to hang pots over the fire.

Potter
Poker. (Lan)

Pottinger
*Porringer.

Pottle
1. Measure of two quarts.
2. A pot, tankard, or other container for drinking.

Pottle Pan, Pot
A pot or tankard holding a *pottle; a drinking vessel.

Pouder
*Pewter.

Pounced
Metalwork that has been ornamentally embossed or chased.

Pouncet Box
Box to hold sand for drying ink, or perhaps for perfume.

Pouncing Iron
Implement for smoothing the nap of a cloth.

Pound
A large trough used for crushing apples in cider-making. (Dev; Con)

Pounder
Pestle; instrument for pounding.

Powder Blue
Powdered smalt, used to whiten linen in the laundry.

Powder Horn
A flask for gun powder, made from the horn of an ox or cow, with a metal or wooden covering.

Powdering
Salting or pickling meat with salt and spices, done in a tub or trough,

Powger
*Porringer.

Pown House
Cider barn. (Dev)

Pows, Powltes
Pulses (peas and beans).

Praised
Appraised, i.e. priced or valued

Praisor
The persons who listed and valued the goods in a probate inventory; the *appraiser.

Prechel
Tool for punching holes in horse-shoes. (War)

Preculae
The beads of a rosary. (Latin)

Presents
The document being read.

Press
1. Large cupboard, with doors, and usually with shelves, for storing clothes, linen, books, etc., sometimes placed in a wall recess. Often the top portion is recessed.
2. *Cheese Press.

Press Bedstead
Bed that folds up into the shape of a *press when not in use.

Press Board
1. Ironing Board. (Ham)
2. Table with a cupboard beneath. (Dby)

Press Cupboard

Wardrobe in which clothes could be hung.

Pressing Iron
Smoothing iron, for ironing clothes.

Pricher
Instrument for punching nails in horse-shoes.

Prick
A goad for oxen.

Prick Song
Music `pricked', i.e. written and sung from the script, rather than by ear or memory.

Pricket
Candlestick with a spike for impaling the candle.

Prig
Small pot or pan of brass or tin. (Yks)

Primella
*Prunella.

Primer
1. Devotional manual or prayer book for use of the laity.
2. Elementary reading book.

Primer Seisen
The right of the crown to receive from the heir of a tenant in chief the first year's income from his estate.

Principal
1. *Mortuary.
2. Main beams and supporting posts of a building.

Print
Mould.

Pritchel
Sharply pointed tool for punching holes; especially used by cobblers, and for punching nail-holes in horse-shoes.

Privy Stool
*Close Barrell.

Processional
Book containing litanies, hymns, etc., for use in processions.

Proctor, Procurator
Lawyer who manages causes in a court of law.

Prongs
Pitchfork.

Prospective Glass
1. Magic glass for seeing the future.
2. Telescope.

Provender Chest
Chest for storing animal feed, kept in a barn or stable.

Prow
Lip, spout, or pointed projections.

Provision
Stock or store of food.

Pruce Chest
Either made of *spruce from Scandinavia, or imported from Prussia.

Prunella
Strong material, originally silk, later worsted; used for the gowns of clergymen, lawyers and graduates.

Pug
A six-month old lamb, or a ewe in its second year.

Puke
Superior type of woollen cloth for making gowns; their bluish-black colour.

Pull Tow
Hemp or tow not worth spinning; the coarse and knotty parts; its refuse. (Sfk)

Pullen
Poultry; domestic fowl.

Puller
Loft for poultry.

Pulses
The edible seeds of leguminous crops such as peas, beans, and vetches; the plants themselves.

Pummice Stone
Used to smooth the surface of parchment.

Pumping Tool
Pump drills for drilling stone and metal; they operated with a pumping action. (Gls)

Punch
A tool for indenting, piercing, or forcing bolts out of holes.

Punch Wood
Wood used for joists, and for the upright timbers of wooden partitions.

Puncheon
1. *Punch.
2. A dagger.
3. *Pancheon.
4. Basket or cask for holding eels.

Pure
Cloth trimmed or cut down to show

one colour only.

Purfle
A border, especially of a garment or cloth embroidered with gold or silver thread, and/or trimmed with pearls, fur, etc.

Purgatory
Receptacle for ashes placed beneath or in front of the fire, which could be used as a milder source of heat than the fire itself. (Sal; Wor)

Purl
Twisted gold or silver thread, used in bordering and embroidery; the loops or twists made by this thread on embroidered cloth.

Purlin
A beam (usually one of two or more) running along the length of a roof, resting on the principal rafters, which it crosses at right angles, and supporting common rafters.

Purparty
Share.

Purr
1. Poker (Dby),
2. Long pole for pushing sheep when being washed.

Put forth; Put to use
Invest.

Putcheon
*Puncheon (4)

Puter, Putor, Putter
*Pewter.

Putt
1. Heavy two-wheeled cart, made to tip. (Dev; Dor)
2. A cask.

Pux
*Pug.

Pyx
Small container holding the consecrated host, suspended over the altar.

Quaife
*Coif.

Qualiver
A light portable gun. (Sry)

Quarrell, Quarry
1. Diamond-shaped or square pane of glass used in *lattice windows.

2. A short heavy square-arrow for a cross-bow.

Quart
A measure of capacity: a quarter of a *gallon or two pints; a pot holding this amount.

Quarter
1. A square panel.
2. The skirt of a coat or other garment. (Oxf)
3. A measure of capacity of grain, eight bushels, but varying by locality.

Quarter Vessel
Containing 25 gallons of liquid. (Wor)

Quartern
1. A quarter of various weights and measures.
2. A vessel holding a quart.

Quarters
Wood four inches wide by two or four inches thick, use as an upright stud or short cross-beam in partitions and other framing.

Queell
Twill; the warp.

Queeling Turn
Device for winding the warp.

Queens Ware
Pale cream-coloured earthenware, originally made by Wedgwood and so-called due to the patronage of Queen Charlotte.

Quern
Small stone hand mill for grinding grain, *malt, mustard, etc. It consisted of two circular stones, rotated one on top of the other.

Quern House
Room for milling.

Quick Goods, Stuff
Live animals.

Quill
A spool on which the weft is wound for placing in the shuttle.

Quill Gold
Gold thread.

Quill Torn, Wheel
The spool of a spinning wheel, on which the weft is wound so that it can be placed in the shuttle.

Quillet
A small plot or strip of land.

Quilling
Winding thread or yarn onto a spool.
Quilt
Made up of a layer of wool, flock, feathers, etc., between two large pieces of material, stitched together. Originally used to lie on, but subsequently as a bed covering.
Quilted Coat
Armoured jacket worn by infantry.
Quilting Frame
Frame on which a counterpane is stretched in the process of quilting.
Quire
Four sheets of paper or parchment folded to form eight leaves; a small book.
Quitclaim
The formal renunciation of a claim, usually relating to property.
Quiver
A case for holding arrows.
Quoin
Wedge shaped block used for various purposes.
Quy
Heifer or female calf up to three years old, or before it has calved. (Northern)
Quystirk
Heifer of one to two years. (Ntt)

Rack
1. An iron bar supporting a spit or cooking utensils.
2. A wooden or metal frame holding animal fodder, which may be in a stable, etc., or in a field.
3. *Tenter.
4. Support for a cross-bow.
5. Framework for storing plates etc.
Rackan
A chain or *rack supporting a pot over the fire.
Rackan Crook, Hook, Team, Tree
Ratcheted iron hook, bar or crane in the chimney, from which *rackans and *pot crooks could be suspended.
Raded, Radden
Made of wattle.
Raddle
The *laths used in wattle and daub buildings.

Radds
Rails of a wain or cart. (Sry)
Radlings
Slender rods, usually of hazel, fastened between upright stakes to form a wall or partition.
Raff
Imported timber, usually in the form of *deal.
Raffle
Wooden instrument used to stir blazing brushwood whilst it was heating an oven. (Nfk)
Ragot
Of variegated design and pattern; patchwork. (Gls)
Raid
*Rave.
Rail
1. A garment: a woman's *neckerchief, shoulder cape, cloak, or jacket.
2. *Rave.
Raiment
Clothing; *apparel.
Rainer
Fine linen made in Rennes, Brittany.
Raised Work
Cloth that has been embossed, or on which a pattern has been cut in the pile.
Rait
1. *Rave.
2. The process of watering hemp or flax by placing it on 'raitles', i.e. racks, in a pond or ditch for some time. (Chs)
Rammel
Brushwood, underwood, etc., especially from trees that have been felled; rubbish. (Northern)
Rammill
Skimmed milk. (Dor)
Randing Knife
For cutting meat into strips. (Gls)
Randlebalk
Wooden beam across a chimney, from which *pot crooks were suspended.
Range, Ranger
1. An iron fire grate, especially one with one or two ovens at its side.
2. Sieve or strainer.
Rape

A crop grown for oil seed.

Rapier

A long, pointed two-edged sword, chiefly designed for thrusting; a small, light sword.

Rash

A smooth fabric made of silk or worsted.

Rasp

A coarse file, with teeth raised on its surface by means of a pointed punch.

Rat Coloured

Dull grey, as used in funeral gowns.

Rat Snatch, Stock

Rat trap.

Rate

A local tax, especially for the church or the poor.

Rath

*Rave.

Ratles

Part of a loom. (Dur)

Ratsbane

Rat poison, especially arsenic.

Rave

1. Rails, framework or shelving which may be attached to the side of a cart to enable a greater load to be carried.

2. The bar on a loom, fitted with teeth, which guides the warp as it is being wound on the beam.

Ray

Dress, attire; kind of striped cloth.

Raying Sieve

Fine-meshed sieve for riddling and cleansing corn.

Readings

A type of coarse cloth.

Ream

Twenty quires, or 480 sheets of paper.

Ream Pot

Cream pot.

Reamer

Vat in which curd is set to harden into cheese.

Reap Hook

Scythe with a curved steel blade and a serrated edge, about eighteen inches long.

Reasons of the Sun

Raisins; sun-dried grapes.

Reckon Crook

Hook in a chimney for hanging cooking pots over the fire.

Recognizance

A bond requiring performance of some obligation, or the payment of a penalty for non-performance.

Red Ochre

An earth much used as a pigment; it consisted of a mixture of hydrated oxide of iron and clay.

Red Sanders

Wood of the East Indies; red sandalwood or rubywood tree, used in dyeing and for medicinal purposes.

Red Wheat

A variety of wheat, reddish in colour.

Red Wood

Generic name for the different types of wood from which various red dyes were extracted.

Reddle

Red ochre for marking sheep.

Reed

1. Wheat straw for thatching.

2. That part of a loom through which warp threads pass.

Reed Wrought Chair

Rush bottomed and backed chair.

Reeing Sieve

A fine sieve of brass or iron, used to ree, that is, to clean grain, pulses, etc.

Reel

1. A framework for winding yarn; the spool of a spinning wheel; sometimes the spinning wheel itself, or a device for spinning without a wheel.

2. A plumb-line or measuring string. (Gls)

Release

A deed conveying property.

Relict

Widow.

Reliquary

Receptacle for the relics of saints, i.e. their bones.

Remainder

The residual interest in an estate when other interests have ended.

Remland, Remlet, Renling

Remainder, residue.

Rennet Pot

Pot to hold rennet, used in cheese-making.

Rep
Fabric of wood, silk or cotton, with a corded surface.

Reparations
Repairs to buildings, fences, etc.

Reparrell, Reppell
*Apparel.

Requiem
Mass said or sung for the repose of the souls of the dead, from the first word of the Latin introit.

Rere Dorter
Area in a monastery behind the *dorter, often used for latrines.

Reredos
1. Ornamental screen of wood or stone covering the wall behind an altar; a curtain used for the same purpose.
2. The back of a brick or stone fireplace; an iron plate forming a fire back.

Rest, Rester
A forked support for a musket used to steady the barrel when firing to ensure greater accuracy of fire; it had a spike to fix it in the ground.

Ret
To soften hemp by soaking it in water, thus dis-engaging the fibres.

Ret Pit
A pit in which flax or hemp was retted.

Reversion
That part of an estate which reverts to the grantor or his representative after the term of the original grant has been completed.

Revolving Churn
*Churn.

Rew
The ridge into which grass falls when cut with a scythe.

Rewer
Rake used to make *rews.

Rial
A gold coin, either Spanish or English, originally worth about ten shillings. First issued in England by Edward IV in 1465.

Rick
A stack of hay, wood, corn, etc., especially one that has been thatched

to keep it dry.

Rick Barton
Enclosure for hay ricks; farmyard.

Rick Staddle, Stavel
Frame of wood placed on *staddle stones or oak posts, on which ricks were built.

Ridder
Course oblong sieve, for winnowing corn.

Rider
A piece of wood with which a pair of harrows are connected.

Riddle
Large, coarse-meshed sieve for separating chaff from grain, sand from gravel, ashes from cinders, etc.

Rider
Piece of wood with which a pair of harrows is connected.

Ridgarth
Type of horse girth. (Chs)

Ridge, Rigg
*Selion or strip of arable in the open field.

Ridgel, Rigeld
An imperfectly castrated animal, or one whose genitals are not perfectly developed.

Riding Beast
Horse.

Riding Cloth
Cloth placed underneath, or instead of, a saddle.

Riding Coat
A long coat, usually deeply divided in the tail.

Riffer
Implement for breaking up rough ground where a plough cannot go.

Rig
Ridge in a ploughed field where sheaves of corn were placed after harvesting.

Rigell
Cloth-making tool. (Dev)

Rigged
Cow with a white stripe on its back.

Rigwiddie
The band, rope, or chain running across the cart saddle on the back of a draught horse to support the shafts of

a cart or carriage. (Bdf)

Ring
1. Cider press.
2. Table mat.
3. Circular pewter plate.
4. Part of a horse's harness.
5. Wooden part in a windmill containing the corn between the stones when grinding.

Ring Bittle
*Beetle with an iron ring around its head.

Ring House
Room or building housing a cider press.

Ringer
1. One who rings church bells; probate records frequently refer to funeral ringers.
2. Crowbar or hammer for driving wedges.

Rip Hook
Reaping hook; scythe with a curved steel blade about 18" long, having a serrated edge.

Ripple
1. *Rave. (Sal)
2. *Rippling Comb.
3. The iron rim on a cart wheel. (Sal)

Rippling Comb, Stock
Instrument toothed like a comb, used to separate seeds from flax or hemp.

Road Saddle
Riding saddle.

Roan
Horse of mixed colour, in which red predominates.

Roan Hood
Hood made with linen from Rouen.

Roasting Iron
*Gridiron used especially for roasting eggs.

Rock, Roke
*Distaff, perhaps with the wool or flax attached to it.

Rock Tree
The long handle by which a blacksmith worked his bellows.

Rodden
Wicker.

Rodmeale
A quarter of an acre.

Roll
1. *Bederoll.
2. Pad to facilitate the carrying of heavy loads, e.g. pails of milk, on the head.
*Roller.

Roller
A heavy cylinder of wood or stone, fitted with shafts or a handle, used for smoothing the ground after ploughing.

Romble
*Rammel.

Rombowline
Poor quality rope or canvas used by seamen for temporary purposes.

Rome
Piece of land. (Dur)

Rood
1. A measure of land area, containing 40 square poles or perches, but varying in different regions.
2. Crucifix, especially one above the screen between the chancel and the nave.

Rood Loft
Loft or gallery above the rood screen in a church upon which the *rood or cross was mounted; also used for an attic in a large house.

Roof Meat
*Flitches, often hung from the roof.

Rook
A heap, stack, or small pile, especially of stones, turf, etc. (Northern)

Rosa Solis
A cordial or liquor, originally made from the juice of the sundew plant, later from spirits and spices.

Rose Nail
Wrought iron nail with a round head facetted by a series of hammer blows, used to secure iron fittings.

Roset
Rose-coloured pigment; a distillation from roses.

Rose Water
Water distilled from roses and used as a perfume.

Rosil
Resin.

Rosin
1. Cobblers wax. (Dur)

2. Adhesive derived from trees. (Lin)

Rother
Horned cattle; an ox.

Rotten Stone
A decomposed siliceous limestone found in the Peak District, used as a powder for polishing metals, etc.

Rough
1. Roof. (Con)
2. Raw, i.e. referring to meat. (Wor)

Rough Mason
Mason who works with unhewn stone.

Round
1. A quantity of material rolled up.
2. A single turn of yarn wound on a reel.
3. A round wooden *trencher.

Round Cloth
Canvas.

Roundabout Chair
Lavishly ornamented chairs with cane-work seats, semi-circular backs and cabriole legs, originally imported from the East Indies via Holland.

Roundel
Ring or hoop holding candles, to hang before a rood or image.

Rove, Roving
Raw, untwisted thread; partially spun worsted.

Rowel
The small wheel with spikes on spurs.

Rowen
Refuse after threshing. (Gls)

Rowle
1. A measure of lard. (Chs)
2. *Rowler.

Rowler
1. Rolling pin.
2. Horse roller, used to crush clods and smooth the ground.

Rowling Stone
Stone *rowler (2).

Rowling Hose
Stockings, the tops of which may be rolled up or down.

Rubber
A hand brush, cloth, etc., used for cleaning and polishing.

Rubber File
Tool for taking the scale off red-hot iron. (Sal)

Ruck
Heap or stack of coal or other fuel, or perhaps of hay.

Rudder
1. *Rother
2. Coarse sieve.
3. Paddle-like utensil for stirring the *malt in the *mashing fat.

Rue Oil
Oil extracted from the rue plant for medicinal purposes.

Ruff, Ruffe
Starched linen frill for neck and wrist wear, crimped or fluted extravagantly, worn by both sexes, but only by the wealthy.

Rug
1. Coverlet (where the word is used in conjunction with other bed-linen).
2. A rough woollen material similar to *frieze, perhaps used as a cloak or a *mantle.

Rugged
Shaggy, rough with hair.

Run Bed
*Truckle Bed.

Run Net
Net which can be run out in a continuous stretch. (Lin)

Runlet
1. Small cask for wine, or for holding the *wort whilst brewing
2. Circular wooden trencher.

Runnel
A small water-course: a ditch, gutter or small stream.

Running Glass
Hour glass.

Running Tub
Tub for rennet.

Runt Oxen
Small breed of oxen; oxen of poor quality.

Rushia Chair
Chairs, either with rush seats, or from Russia, upholstered in *Russia leather.

Russell
A ribbed or corded woollen fabric, probably of Flemish origin.

Russet
Coarse home-spun woollen cloth, usually of a reddish-brown colour, used

by country people for clothing; the colour itself.

Russia Leather
Durable, light leather, made from skins cured using oil derived from birch bark, and often used for book bindings.

Rydge Withes
*Rigwiddie

Rylle
Rivulet, small stream, or brook.

Sack
1. Cloth often used for window covering.
2. A bag made of coarse flax or hemp for the storage of dry goods; a measure of the quantity of goods, e.g. hops, corn, flour, etc.
3. Dry white wine imported from Spain and the Canaries.

Sack Cloth
A coarse fabric used for making bags and sacks.

Sackhouse
A wine cellar.

Sad
1. Dull or dark; a sombre colour.
2. In relation to metal-ware, solid, dense, heavy.
3. Serious.

Sad Iron
A solid smoothing iron, for ironing cloth.

Sad Ware
Heavy or dark-coloured goods, especially metalware such as pots, chargers, fire backs, etc.

Saddle Tree
Framework of a saddle; the block on which it was shaped.

Safe
Food cupboard, or chest, with sides of woven hair allowing ventilation, but keeping out flies and other insects: an *aumbry.

Safeguard
Outer skirt or petticoat, worn by women over their kirtle as a protection against dirt when riding.

Sagathy
Woollen worsted fabric.

Sage
*Swage.

Sage Cheese
Cheese flavoured and mottled by liquid pressed from sage leaves.

Sag Chair
Rush seated chair, i.e. sedge.

Salamander
Circular iron plate attached to a long handle, placed in a fire until red hot, then used to brown pastry, omelettes, etc.

Sallet
1. A close-fitting armoured helmet with a protective backpiece, and perhaps with a vizor, made of steel.
2. An iron vessel.
3. A salad dish.

Saloon
The principal reception room in a gentleman's house.

Salt, Salt Pie, Pitch
A container or box for salt and other condiments; a salt cellar, or perhaps a block of salt.

Salt Box, Cote, House
Box or room for storing salt, or perhaps the place where it is produced.

Salt Victuals
Meat salted for preservation.

Salter
Psalter, i.e. the book of Psalms.

Salting
Curing meat or fish using salt.

Salting Bench, Cowl, Kimnel, Store, Trough, Tub
Bench, *kimnel, *cowl (2), trough or tub used for salting meat or fish.

Salvatory
Box to hold ointments.

Salver
A broad flat piece of plate, usually with a foot, used as a tray.

Sameron
Cloth with a texture between linen and hemp. (Dur; Yks)

Samphire
Plant with fleshy leaves used in pickles.

Sampler
Piece of embroidered canvas.

Sanctuary
*Glebe.

Sand Box
Box with a perforated lid used to sprinkle sand on wet ink as a blotter to dry it.

Sand Sack
Sack for carrying sand from the beach to use as fertilizer. (Con)

Sandalwood, Sanders
A scented wood rendering a yellow or red dye; *red sanders.

Sandaric
Red arsenic sulphide.

Sandiver
Saline liquid found on glass after vitrification; glass gall.

Sap
Type of spade or mattock.

Sap Lath
A *lath made of sapwood.

Sarcenet
A very fine soft material, used for hangings, blinds and furniture covers.

Sarch
*Searce .

Sarcophagus
Piece of equipment, e.g. a wine cooler, a grate, in the shape of an Egyptian sarcophagus.

Sarger
A fine sieve or strainer. (Dev)

Sarpe
Collar or neck ring of gold or silver.

Sarplier
A large canvas sack for wool or other merchandise, containing 80 tods.

Sarsaparilla
Tonic derived from the dried roots of a South American tree.

Sarsenet
A very fine soft silk, used for quilts, linings, bed *hangings, etc.

Sasafras
Dried bark of a North American tree, used medicinally.

Sash Line
Sash cord for opening and closing windows; sash windows were introduced at the end of the 17th c.

Satin
Silk fabric with a glossy surface on one side.

Satinisco
An inferior quality satin.

Saucepan
Small *skillet, with a long handle, for boiling sauces.

Saucer
Sauceboat, usually metal, used for holding sauces and condiments; they were not used to hold cups until the 18th c.

Saunders
*Sandalwood

Save All
Candlestick used for burning candle ends.

Saving Iron
1. Iron plate or fender to protect the coal from the heat of the fire. (Dev)
2. Dripping pan. (Dev)

Say
1. Fine cloth, similar to serge, formerly partly of silk, but subsequently entirely woollen, and used for bedding and wall hangings, table coverings, etc.
2. Bucket with two ears, through which a pole may be passed to make a handle for one or two to carry.

Scabbard
Sheath or case for a sword, protecting the blade.

Scabellum
Stool or bench. (Latin)

Scaffold
*Staddle

Scala Caeli
Chapel or altar to which an indulgence was attached; originally the name of a church near Rome to which the same indulgence was attached.

Scalding Tub
Early form of sterilizer for cleansing utensils, especially those used in the dairy.

Scale Baulk
The bar of a balance.

Scallop
In the shape of a shell.

Scammony
Gum resin from convovulus roots, used as a strong purgative.

Scamnum
A bench. (Latin)

Scavilones

Long drawers worn under the *hose by men.

Scellett, Scillett
*Skillet

Scia
The sleeve-opening of a gown. (Dur)

Scoath
Pole, bar or forked stick. (Dur)

Scollop
Rod used to fasten down thatch on roofs: a thatch peg.

Scomer
*Skimmer

Sconce
1. Candle holder, perhaps fitted to a wall, and perhaps with a screen to protect the flame. In wealthy households it would have a polished backplate or mirror to reflect the light.
2. Screen, partition, seat or stone shelf in the kitchen.
3. Kitchen utensil set before the fire.

Sconce Glass
Looking glass fitted with sockets to hold candles.

Scoop
Joint of mutton or beef. (Dev)

Scoot
Small piece of ground, the corner of a field.

Scopper
A tool used for hollowing out portions of the surface being worked upon (Dur)

Score
Account for goods obtained on credit.

Scotch Cap
Head gear made of thick woollen cloth, without a brim, decorated with tails or streamers.

Scotch Cloth
Linen supposedly woven with nettle fibres: cheap fabric resembling *lawn.

Scraw
1. A scroll or tag of parchment or leather.
2. Frame on which fabric is hung to dry.

Screel
1. Wooden bucket or tub for holding water or milk. (Lin)
2. Screen for dressing corn. (Lin; Yks)

Screen
1. A movable partition, perhaps for stopping draughts, or for protection from the heat of a fire.
2. A *settle. (Lan)
3. A wire sieve on a frame, used to separate grain from chaff, dust and other impurities.
4. A marking iron. (Dev)
5. A cloth-making tool. (Dev)

Screen Bench
A wooden seat or *settle with a high back to keep out draughts.

Screen Mill
Apparatus for sifting *malt. (Dev)

Screw Plate
A hardened steel plate used by smiths to cut screw threads; it has tapped holes of various diameters drilled in it.

Screw Press
Press such as a cider or cheese press, operated by a screw.

Scribbling
The first stage in the treatment of fleece wool, in which the fibres are straightened before carding begins.

Scriptor
Bureau or desk with shelves for books, and drawers; an *escritoire.

Scrivenor
A *notary or copyist; one who drafts or copies documents such as wills, *bonds, deeds, etc.

Scrub
A breed of cattle distinguished by their small size.

Scrutor
*Escritoire.

Scull
*Skull.

Scullery
Small back kitchen.

Scummer
*Skimmer.

Scuppet
Broad wooden shovel often made from willow, used by maltsters and hop driers.

Scutcheon
*Escutcheon.

Scuttle
1. Winnowing implement; either a

wicker basket or a bowl, in which the grain could be agitated, or a shovel to toss it in the air, so that the wind could separate the wheat from the chaff.

2. A large basket used for carrying corn, earth, vegetables, etc.

3. A dish or *trencher.

Scythe

A tool for mowing grass and other crops; it has a long, thin, curving blade, fastened at an angle to a wooden handle, and wielded with both hands in a long, sweeping stroke.

Sea Card

Marine chart.

Sea Coal

Coal. The name is usually explained by the fact that London was supplied with coal by sea from Newcastle upon Tyne. But not all sea coal was carried by sea, and this explanation has been questioned.

Seal

Rope or chain for tying animals up. (Nfk)

Seal of Arms

A signet engraved with the heraldic arms of the owner.

Sealed, Sealing

1. Walls which have been lined or overlaid with panelling or *wainscot.

2. Rooms which have had a ceiling installed, hiding the rafters, and perhaps covering the floor boards of an upper storey.

3. Furniture such as beds and chairs which are panelled, with a solid frame.

Seam

1. A packhorse load or cartload.

2. A measure of corn.

3. Fat, grease, hog's lard.

Seaman's Needle

Compass.

Seam Pannier

Basket for carrying fat or grease.

Seaming Lace

Lace inserted into, or covering and ornamenting, seams in clothing or fabric.

Seamster

One engaged in fine sewing for a livelihood.

Searce, Search

1. A fine sieve, which might be made of sheepskin in which small holes had been drilled, and used for sifting flour; alternatively, it might be made of bristles or cloth and used in the dairy.

2. A tool for nicking wrought iron or steel. (Sal)

Seat

1. A piece of leather forming the foundation for a heel in boots and shoes.

2. A pillion for a woman, fastened behind the saddle.

3. A blacksmith's tool used for cutting iron.

Seblet

*Seedlip.

Sedge

Coarse grasses much used for making chairs, brushes, etc.

Seed Cod, Cot, Hope

*Seedlip.

Seedlip

A basket shaped to fit the waist, with a shoulder strap, used to carry seed when it is being sown.

Seeing Glass

Looking glass or mirror.

Seeler

Tapestry canopy or covering for a bed. (War)

Seg

1. *Sedge.

2. An animal which has been castrated when fully grown, e.g. a bull, a pig, a sheep.

Seized

In legal possession of property.

Selion

One of several parallel strips of land in an open field, lying between two furrows.

Sell

A low seat or stool. (Ham)

Sellar

*Cellar: a store room, not necessarily underground.

Seller of Bottles

Case or stand for holding bottles.

Sellepp, Selliop

*Seedlip.

Semmet
Implement used in winnowing. (Dev)
Sempiternum
Twilled woollen stuff, similar to
*perpetuana.
Sendal
Thin silken material.
Senight
Seven nights; a week.
Senvy
Mustard seed.
Serge
A woollen fabric, whose precise nature
has varied over time. Originally it was
used for *hangings (2), bed coverings,
etc.; from the 16th c., it was worn by
the poorer classes on account of its
durability; subsequently a durable,
twilled worsted fabric.
Seron
Bale of exotic products, e.g. almonds,
cocoa, etc., encased in an animal's
hide.
Serpentine
Type of cannon, often used as a ship's
gun in the 15th and 16th centuries.
Serpentine Powder
Gunpowder for use with a *serpentine.
Serrandole
Type of candlestick or candelabra.
Serve
A shallow basket used for a horse's
feed. (Wor)
Sess
A local tax or levy.
Sester
A measure of beer or wine; a vessel for
holding that measure.
Set
1. Jewellery set on a garment.
2. A squared stone used for paving.
3. Tool used as a punch for rivetting.
4. A large piece of coal.
5. Jack for lifting the *axletree of a
waggon or carriage
Set Iron
A bar of soft iron.
Set Pot
Iron cauldron set in stone or brick
above a grate, used for boiling clothes.
Set Work
Stitching or embroidery used in

tapestry.
Seth
Sieve or milk-strainer. (Dur)
Setter
Net or trap for catching or killing
birds.
Setting Net
Net used for catching rabbits, hares,
etc., or a fishing net for setting across
a stream.
Setting Stick
1. A stick or dibble used to make holes
for `setting' plants.
2. A rod used in making the pleats of
*ruffs.
Settle
1. Long wooden bench, with a
high back, arms, and cupboards
underneath, capable of seating several
people
2. Raised shelf or frame, of brick or
wood, for supporting barrels or milk
cans.
Settle Bed
Bed which folds into a *settle .
Severalty
Land held by one individual in a
consolidated, enclosed area of land, as
opposed to scattered strips in the open
field held in common.
Sewstern
*Cistern.
Shack Fork
Wooden fork for shaking corn out of
straw. (Dby)
Shackles
1. Iron links connecting the plough
beam to the swingletree.
2. *Horse lock.
Shaft
The long slender rod of an arrow.
Shag
Thick piled, long haired cloth, usually
worsted, with a velvet nap on one side.
Shagreen
Leather made from horse hide, dyed
green, and used to cover small boxes
and cases, etc.
Shake Fork
A wooden fork with two prongs used
by threshers to shake and separate the
straw from the grain.

Shalloon
A closely woven woollen cloth often used for linings.

Shallop
Sloop: a large, heavy boat, with one or more masts, and sometimes with guns.

Shambles
Place where animals were slaughtered.

Shamey
Chamois: a soft pliable leather originally from the skin of the chamois (a species of antelope), but subsequently obtained from the skins of sheep, goats, deer, calves, etc.

Shank
Fur obtained from the legs of animals, especially kids, goats, or sheep, used to trim outer garments.

Shank Pan
Small pan with a long handle. (Dur)

Share
1. *Plough Share.
2. *Shears.

Shaul
A wooden scoop used for winnowing corn. (Ssx)

Shave
Tool for smoothing or paring wood.

Sheal
Husk of oats, wheat, etc.

Shear Board
Padded board on which cloth was stretched for cropping with hand-shears.

Shear Hog, Shear Wether
Sheep after first shearing.

Shearing Knife
A broad bladed tool to cut the edges of thatch.

Shearman
One who shears woollen cloth.

Shears
A term applied to various implements resembling a large pair of scissors, e.g. for cutting cloth, for shearing sheep, etc.

Sheat
A pig under a year old.

Shed
The opening of the warp threads through which the weft shuttle passes.

Sheder

A lamb of 8 months plus, prior to its first shearing. (Lin; Yks)

Sheede, Sheedle
Rough wooden implement or pole. (Dev)

Sheep Bar
1. Hurdles used for sheep folds.
2. *Sheep rack.

Sheep Hook
A shepherd's crook.

Sheep Mark
Implement for making marks of ownership on sheep.

Sheep Rack
1. Hurdle on which sheep were held whilst being shorn.
2. A rack from which sheep feed.

Sheer
1. A crop of grass.
2. The quantity of wool cut from an entire flock in one season.
3. The part of a waggon to which the shafts are attached.
4. A sheath.
5. A *plough share.

Sheers
1. *Shears.
2. Coal tongs. (Gls)

Shelboard
*Raves.

Sheorbo
*Theorbo

Shield Board
The mould board of a plough.

Sheppick
Pitch fork with tines set widely apart and a short handle.

Shetlock
Crosspiece at the back of a waggon into which the tailboard is fitted. (Wil)

Shide
A plank or thin board.

Shift
The division of the open field with a view to rotating crops.

Shilling
Silver coin worth twelve pence.

Ship
In ecclesiastical contexts, a container for incense.

Ship Scraper
Instrument for scraping the keels and

decks of ships.

Shippon
Cattle shed or cow house.

Shirt Band
Shirt collar, *ruff, or wrist-band.

Shive
1. Bung for stopping casks.
2. Small iron wedge fastening the bolt of a window shutter.

Shod, Shoed
Furnished with a shoe of metal, e.g. cart wheels rimmed with iron, shovels edged with metal, etc.

Shoeing
The metal tyre of a wheel.

Shoeing Box
Frame for controlling horses when being shod.

Shole, Showle
Shovel.

Shoot
1. An open trough.
2. A litter of pigs.

Shooter
Board placed between cheeses when in the press.

Shooting Staff
Arrow.

Shop
The work-place of a craftsman; place where business was conducted.

Shop Board
Table or counter on which business was transacted, or goods displayed.

Shop Book
Account book for recording trading debts.

Shop Stuff
Stock in trade.

Shorllings Skynes
Sheep skins after fleeces have been shorn.

Shot
1. Young pig that has been weaned.
2. An idle worthless youth.
3. Ill grown ewe; the animals left when the best of the flock have been selected.
4. A fabric with warp threads of one colour, and weft threads of another.

Shotchill
*Shuttle

Shoull, Showle
Shovel.

Shove
Large fork used to pick up oats when harvesting.

Shovel Board
*Shuffleboard.

Shovel Tree
The handle of a spade or shovel.

Shrapnet
Snare or trap for birds, baited with corn. (Ess)

Shred
A coverlet.

Shreds
Shredded fabric used as stuffing for *beds (1), pillows, and *bolsters (1).

Shredding
Prunings or loppings of trees and undergrowth.

Shredden Heling
Patchwork coverlet.

Shrine
Box or coffer.

Shroud
1. The ropes attached to the top of a ship's mast.
2. Sheet in which a corpse is wrapped for burial.

Shruff
Waste wood for the fire; also applied to old brass or copper.

Shuffleboard
Table for a game in which a coin is driven by the blow of a hand across a highly polished surface, marked with transverse lines.

Shut
1. Bar or bolt to lock the door.
2. Shutter.

Shuttle
Spool carrier in a weaver's loom; used for shuttling the *weft between the threads of the warp.

Side Bedstead
A bedstead which fitted against the wall, and therefore had only two posts, rather than four.

Side Saddle
Lady's saddle made so that both feet are on the same side of the horse.

Sideboard

Table fixed against a wall, for eating, or for the display of household plate; later ones had cupboards and drawers, etc., and the display function became more important.

Sie Boul
Bowl to be used with a *searce when straining liquids, especially milk.

Sile
1. *Sile Dish.
2. One of a pair of main timbers in a timber-framed house.

Sile Dish
Wooden strainer with a linen bottom for straining milk.

Silk Frame
Frame on which silk is stretched to be embroidered.

Sill
*Thill (Dby; Yks)

Sillatory
*Still (2). (War)

Silt
Trough for salting meat.

Silver Foin
Silver hammered into thin sheets.

Silver Gilt
Silver plated with a thin layer of gold.

Silver Nut
Cup made from a coconut shell mounted in silver.

Silver Stone
1. Jewellery set in silver.
2. Stoneware jug with a silver rim.

Sime
Straw rope or cord holding down the thatch of hay stacks, etc. (Northern)

Simnel
Bread or bun made from fine flour; a rich currant cake, traditionally eaten on the mid-Sunday in Lent.

Simple
Medicine.

Simple Pot
A pot for *simples or medicines.

Sin
A strainer or sieve. (Dur)

Sink Stone
Stone basin in a kitchen with a pipe attached, where dishes were washed, and where water could drain away.

Sinker

Circular lid of a *cheese press, which presses the curds down to form the cheese. (Northern)

Sippets
Small chunks of bread, perhaps toasted or fried, eaten with soup or *posset.

Sir
Title applied to clergy until the Reformation.

Sisers
Scissors. (Dev)

Sisters Thread
Bleached thread.

Sithorne
*Cithern.

Sivet, Sivil
Square iron bar or buckle beside a *saddle tree, on which to hang girth straps or stirrup leathers.

Skale
Wooden cup or goblet. (Dby)

Skeel
Wooden tub or bucket for milk or water; the handles were formed by staves projecting above the rim.

Skein
Thread or yarn wound to a certain length on a reel.

Skelboose, Skelbuse
Front boards of a cow stall. (Lin; Yks)

Skele
Dish or platter. (War)

Skelf
Shelf. (Dur)

Skellat
A small hand bell, used for ecclesiastical purposes, or by a bell-man. (Lin)

Skene
Knife or dagger.

Skeining Wheel
Wheel for winding wool into skeins.

Skep
1. Beehive made of straw.
2. Basket or hamper for grain or coal.
3. Bowl-shaped vessel with handles for ladling.

Skey
One of a pair of wooden bars at each end of an ox-yoke, to which the neck-straps are attached. (Dur)

Skeys of Sherops

Cloth-making tools. (Dev)

Skile
Thin, shallow vessel for skimming milk. (Lin)

Skillet
1. A metal pan with three or four short legs and a long handle, used for boiling or stewing over an open fire; a large *posnet.
2. A pan without legs, similar to a frying pan or sauce pan, and made of brass or copper. (Sal)

Skimmer
1. Flat perforated metal ladle for removing scum or fat from boiling liquids, or for skimming cream from milk; a cooking ladle.
2. Fire shovel or scoop for raking ashes.

Skin Wool
Wool from the skin of a dead sheep.

Skip
1. *Skep (2).
2. Small utensil for taking up yeast.
3. A child's long gown.

Skiver
Skewer, used to fasten meat together whilst being cooked.

Skull
A close fitting armoured helmet.

Slab Board
Rough sap-wood plank with bark on one side, cut from a log when it was first squared up.

Slat
Narrow strip of wood or stone used for roofing.

Slaughter Cradle
Pen in which animals were slaughtered.

Slay, Sley
The wooden frame holding the reed and driving home the weft; the handboard of a loom.

Slay Silk
Silk thread for embroidery, which can be separated into smaller filaments.

Sled, Sledge
1. A flat bottomed truck which slid over the ground, used for transporting heavy goods; often used in harvesting on steep slopes, where a low centre of gravity was essential, or for transporting ploughs.
2. Sledge hammer used by blacksmiths for beating iron on an anvil.

Sled Bridle
Harness for a *sled.

Sleekstone
A smooth stone used for smoothing and polishing.

Sleeper
Wooden beam used as a support for a wall or floor, etc. in a building.

Slice
1. Collective term for a variety of flattish cooking utensils, e.g. a spatula.
2. Fire shovel, used particularly for taking ashes out of bread ovens. Its end was shaped like a spade or paddle.

Sling Trace
The chains or ropes connecting the horse's collar to the *swingletree.

Sling Tree
*Swingle tree.

Slink Skin
The skin of an aborted or premature calf or other animal. (Hrt)

Slip
1. Spoon handle with its top cut off obliquely.
2. A measure of yarn.
3. A young pig.
4. A counterfeit coin made of brass, but washed over with silver. (Dev)

Slip Sconce
A long or elongated *sconce.

Slipe
The iron shoe of a plough.

Slipping
Large skein of spun thread or yarn.

Slivered Wool
A continuous strand of wool in a loose, untwisted condition, ready for *slubbing preparatory to spinning.

Slob Bench
Working surface for use when handling liquids. (Sal)

Slop Basin
Utensil for tea leaves.

Slubbing
Removing lumpy imperfections from *slivered wool.

Slugg
Heavy piece of crude metal.

Small Beer
Beer of a weak or inferior quality.
Smiths Coal
1. Charcoal.
2. *Coal.
Smock
1. A woman's undergarment; a shift.
2. A man's loose outer garment, worn by farm labourers instead of a coat, and reaching the knees.
Smoke Jack
Fan in a flue, which revolved in the rising smoke, and powered a revolving spit; see *jack .
Smoothing Box
*Ironing Box.
Smoothing Iron
Implement for ironing clothes.
Snaffle
A simple form of bridle bit, without a curb.
Snath, Snead
Crooked shaft or handle of a scythe.
Sneck
A latch.
Snett
Deer fat. (Ess)
Snip
Horse with a white patch on its nostril or lip.
Snuffer
Scissors for snuffing out candles and trimming their wicks, with a closed box to hold the charred wick.
Snype
Poor, boggy pasture. (Dur)
Soa, Soe
Large round tub for brewing, or washing clothes in. Not to be confused with sow, i.e. female pig.
Soale
*Plough share. (Dev)
Sock
*Plough share
Soe
1. *Say (2).
2. *Soa.
Socage
A form of tenure in which the tenant was free in status and had few obligations.
Sods

Rough saddle made of coarse cloth or skin stuffed with straw. (Dur)
Soil
Human excrement used as manure.
Solar
An upper room, or loft often with a large window to catch the sunlight.
Sole
Rope, chain, or wooden yoke placed around the neck of cattle to fasten them to their stall. (Dur)
Soling Leather
Leather for making shoe soles.
Solve
*Sull. (Dev)
Sommer
*Sumpter horse.
Sore
*Sorrel .
Sorrel
1. Bright chestnut colour; often a horse of this colour.
2. Herb used in salads and cookery, or as a medicine.
Soome, Some
Chain or rope attaching a draught animal to a waggon, plough, etc. (Dur)
Sorry
Decrepit, old, of little value, poor.
Soul Scot
Payment due to the church on the death of a person; a *mortuary.
Sow
1. Female pig.
2. Bar or ingot of some metal.
3. Mould for cast iron.
Sowel
1. A plough with a *sole to which the *share is attached.
2. Hurdle stake. (Dor)
Sowl
A wash tub.
Spane
To wean. (Dur)
Spaning Calf, Pig
Weaning calf or pig. (Ntt; Yks)
Spanish Brown
Type of earth yielding a reddish-brown pigment.
Spanish Leather
Fine leather originally made in Cordoba.

Spanish Money
Foreign coins circulated widely in
England in the early modern period.
Spanish Table
Portable table that folds up.
Spar
1. A thatching rod, made of split
willow, pointed and twisted double.
2. A piece of timber, perhaps a rafter,
or a large bolt for a door.
Sparable, Sparrow Bill
Small, headless, wedge-shaped nail
used in shoe-making.
Spark
Fragment; remnant.
Sparver
A canopy for a bed or cradle.
Spatter
Spatula.
Spatterdash, Splatterdash
Long cloth, leather leggings, or gaiters,
to prevent trousers or stockings being
spattered with dirt when riding.
Spattle Staff
The handle of a spade.
Speak
Piece of wood used to keep thatch in
place.
Spear
Screen between the door and the
fireplace to keep out draughts. (Sry)
Specet
*Specialty.
Specialty
A sealed *bond or *obligation, often
entered into as security for a loan or
debt.
Specie
Coin; coined money.
Speer
Wooden framed screen on the inside
of a door or by the fire to keep out
draughts; if made of wainscot they
were termed *portals. On the inside, a
*settle and a shelf might be attached.
Spence
A service room: a pantry, larder,
buttery, etc., or perhaps a cupboard or
a container for milk.
Sperate Debt
Debt likely to be recovered, perhaps
under a *specialty or *obligation.

Spermaceti
A fatty substance derived from sperm
whale, used to make candles, and for
medicinal purposes.
Spetch
A strip or patch of leather, perhaps
used for mending shoes.
Spialty
*Specet.
Spigot, Spile, Spill
Wooden stopper for the vent-hole of a
cask or barrel.
Spikenard
An aromatic substance.
Spill
Part of a plough. (Dev)
Spill Press
Press for finishing cloth, using `spills'
i.e. interleaved paper. (Dev)
Spill Wood
Wood refuse `spilt' by sawyers.
Spindle
1. The earliest hand device for
spinning wool, which puts the twist
in the yarn and carries it round on its
shank.
2. An iron rod acting as an axle, used
with *grinding stones.
Spindle Chair
Arm chair made mainly of spindles, i.e.
cylindrical wooden bars.
Spindle Whorl
The small round weight at the lower
end of a *spindle which acted as a fly-
wheel.
Spinet
A keyed musical instrument, similar to
a harpsichord, but smaller and single-
stringed.
Spinked
Speckled, spotted. (Yks)
Spinning
Spun thread or yarn.
Spinning Turn
*Turn.
Spinster
A woman who spins, especially one
whose usual occupation this is; not
necessarily a single woman.
Spire
*Portal. (Oxf)
Spit

A thin revolving bar thrust through meat and stood on *cobirons in front of the open fire, for roasting.

Spital
House for the poor or diseased; a hospital.

Spitter
A spade.

Spittle Spade
Small spade.

Spitting Sheet
Small sheet of linen at the bedside for spitting into.

Spitting Tub, Box
Spittoon; receptacle for spit, usually round and flat, of earthenware or metal and sometimes with a cover in the shape of a funnel.

Splints
Flexible armour made of small overlapping plates to protect the arms and elbows.

Splot
Plot or small piece of land.

Spokeshave
A small plane, with slightly curved blade, used by carpenters, coopers, wheel-wrights, etc., to shape barrel staves, spokes, etc.

Spoking Chain
Used to fit spokes to a wheel.

Sponge
1. Long narrow strip of enclosed land. (Sfk)
2. Ground of a swampy or boggy nature.

Spooling Swift
A light reel on which a skein of silk is placed to be wound off. (Oxf)

Spoon Mould
Tinker's mould for making spoons.

Spreeding Sheet
Bed covering.

Sprigged
Cloth patterned with flowers or leaves, which might be embroidered, woven, or stamped; also applied to ceramic ware.

Spring
1. A copse or wood where young trees are growing from old stools.
2. A plantation, especially one

enclosed for keeping game.

Spring Saw
A bow saw.

Spring Tree
*Swingletree.

Sprit
Nautical term for a small boom or pole which crosses the sail of a boat diagonally from the mast to the upper corner of the sail.

Spruce
Goods imported from Prussia and the Baltic, especially spruce leather, used for making jerkins; spruce fir, often used for making coffers and boxes, etc.; spruce ochre, a yellow or orange-brown pigment.

Spud
A digging implement with a narrow chisel-shaped blade.

Spung
A purse.

Spur
1. Short supporting timber.
2. Foot device to prick a horse to urge it forward.

Spur Royal
Gold coin minted under James I, worth fifteen shillings; a device on one side resembled a *rowel, hence the name.

Spurging Tub
Tub for fermenting beer.

Spurling
Type of sprat; may also refer to the nets used to catch them.

Spy Glass
Early type of telescope.

Squab
1. Originally thick, soft cushions, but later applied to sofas or couches.
2. Club like feet on furniture.

Squirm
Yarn was placed on a squirm when it came from being spun; it was wound from the squirm to the warping bar.

Stack
1. Hay, straw, grain in the sheaf, etc., piled into a square or circular stack and thatched to protect it from the weather.
2. A measure of coal and wood.

Stack Bar

Hurdle for fencing a *stack (1).

Stack Garth
Rick or stack yard.

Stack Stones
*Staddle stones used as the base of a *rick staddle.

Stack Wood
A load of faggot firewood.

Staddle
Raised platform on which ricks were built, to keep the crop off the ground and protect it against rodents.

Staddle Stone
Tapered stone pillar with a cap, in the shape of a mushroom; a number were needed to form a *staddle.

Staff Hook
Long-handled hook or sickle, used to cut peas and beans, and to trim hedges.

Stag
A male animal in its prime, especially an unbroken stallion or a young *ox.

Stag Horn
Deer antler used as knife handle.

Stained Canvas, Cloth
*Painted cloth

Stake
1. Small, movable anvil.
2. Timber or plank supporting a hay rick.
3. Steel clothing; armour. (Oxf)

Stalder
Stool on which casks were placed.

Stale
The handle of a broom or other implement.

Stall
Hive, or stock of bees for a hive.

Stall Cloth
Bench-cloth, especially for a bench in front of a shop on which goods are displayed for sale.

Stallage
A barrel stand.

Stamen
The warp thread of a textile fabric.

Stamin
A coarse worsted fabric, originally made in Norfolk.

Stammel
A coarse worsted cloth, or *linsey woolsey, usually dyed red; the colour itself.

Stammet
Cloth, perhaps fulled, and usually dyed red.

Stamp
Instrument for making holes in horse-shoes.

Stamped Paper
Paper, vellum, or parchment on which a duty introduced in 1694 had been levied, and which was stamped accordingly.

Stamper
Copper mallet for beating felt placed on a *block into the shape of a hat.

Stand
1. Stall for a horse or ox. (Lin)
2. Wooden vessel to hold *small beer. (Lan)

Stand Cratch, Heck
Fodder rack, standing on four posts, for use in the field or yard.

Standard
1. A measuring vessel.
2. A tall candlestick.
3. A stand, on a single pillar, with a branched foot, used as the base for a washing basin, a dressing table, a candlestick, etc.
4. Permanent fixtures and fittings to remain in a house, treated as inalienable chattels.
5. A chest used when travelling. (Dby)
6. A tree standing alone or above the underwood, especially one that has not been coppiced.

Stander, Standert
1. A frame for supporting barrels, pails, kits, etc.
2. A barrel set on its end, an open tub.

Standing
Fixed.

Standing Bedstead
A high bedstead on legs under which a *truckle bed could be rolled; a four-poster with a *tester, curtains, and *valance.

Standing Cup
A cup with a stem and a foot to stand on; frequently valuable plate.

Standing Cupboard

A wardrobe that stands on its base.

Standing Desk

*Desks with sloping lids and legs.

Standing Press

*Standing Cupboard.

Standish

A stand or tray for writing materials; an ink-stand.

Stang

1. A wooden beam or bar, which might have various different uses, e.g. the side of a cart, the beam to which the harness is attached, the side piece of a ladder, to hang *flitches on, etc.
2. An eel spear.
3. A rood of land. (Lin; Yks)

Staple

A thread of wool, especially as regards its length and fineness.

Start

A handle. (Lin)

Statute Lace

Lace woven according to statute for those forbidden to wear foreign lace.

Stavesacre

A plant whose seeds were used as an emetic, or to destroy vermin.

Stays

Corsets.

Steane

1. Clay vessel with two handles or ears, used for storing food or liquids.
2. Box carrying stones used to press down on curds in cheese-making; a cheese-press. (Dor)
3. An earthenware drinking vessel.

Stechados

French lavender, used medicinally.

Steddy

*Stithy.

Stee

Ladder. (Northern)

Steech

Stooks: a dozen or so sheaves stacked in a field. (Dev)

Steed

*Bedstead.

Steel

1. A sharp cutting tool or weapon.
2. A bar or rod of steel used for sharpening knives.

Steel Cap

Skull cap of steel worn by infantry soldiers.

Steel Glass

Glass backed with steel to make a mirror, or perhaps a mirror made of polished steel.

Steel Mill

1. A *malt mill
2. Device for producing a stream of sparks by rotating a steel disk against a flint.

Steelyard

A type of balance, used particularly for weighing meat. The balance had unequal arms; the counterweight was slid along the longer one until equilibrium was reached and the weight of the object measured.

Steep Lead, Steeping Vat

Vat for steeping, used in brewing, dyeing, or clothes washing.

Steer

Young castrated bull; an ox.

Steg

A gander. (Yks)

Stell

A stand for barrels; trestles.

Startup

Originally a type of boot or shoe worn by rustics that `started' in the middle of the leg; subsequently, gaiters.

Stew

1. Hatter's drying room.
2. Heated room; room with a fireplace.
3. Cooking vessel or *cauldron.

Steyney

Earthenware pan.

Stibium

Black antimony, used as a cosmetic for blackening the eyebrows, or as an emetic or poison.

Stick

A measure of the length of a roll of fabric imported from Flanders.

Stiddy

*Stithy.

Stile

1. *Still (2).
2. Upright post or bar in *wainscot panelling.

Stile Iron

Iron for pressing clothes.
Stiled Dog
Iron fire-dog. (Dev)
Stiletto
A short dagger, with a thick blade in proportion to its length.
Still, Stilt
1. Stand for a barrel or tub.
2. Apparatus for distilling.
3. *Cooler.
Still House
Room or building with a *still (2).
Stillatory
*Still (2), or place for distilling.
Stilliard
*Steelyard
Stilt
The handle of a plough. (Dur)
Sting
A pole, post, shaft, etc. (Dur)
Stint
The number of beasts that a farmer is allowed to have on common land.
Stirk
Young bullock or heifer, usually one to two years old.
Stitch
Sheaves stacked temporarily in the harvest field.
Stithy
Blacksmith's anvil.
Stock
1. The block of wood on which a butcher cuts his meat, a fishmonger cuts fish, or on which food is prepared.
2. A stand, frame, or ledge for placing churns, basins, etc.
3. A trough or basin.
4. Collective name for a tradesman's goods, or for a farm's animals.
5. A swarm of bees; their hive.
6. The heavy part of a tool, implement or weapon, e.g. the frame of a spinning wheel, the wooden portion of a gun, the handle of a whip.
7. The hub of a wheel.
8. A stiff, close-fitting neckcloth.
Stock Axe
Similar to a pick axe, but with the blades flattened for cutting.
Stock Bed
*Bed stock

Stock Card
Wool *card fastened to a stock (6) or support, thus leaving both hands free to comb.
Stock Fish
Fish, especially cod, dried without salting.
Stock Lock
Lock for an outer door, fitted in a wooden case.
Stock Stool
Stool made from a tree-trunk or large log.
Stocks and Blocks
Odds and ends.
Stoddle
Loom. (Nth)
Stomacher
Ornamental covering for a woman's chest, worn under the lattice of a *bodice; bib of an apron; a type of waistcoat for men.
Stone, Stonige, Stoning, Stony
Made of stone; in the South-West, usually moorstone.
Stone Blue
Compound of indigo and starch or whiting, used in laundering.
Stone Bow
Cross-bow or catapult that shoots stones, used to kill birds or small animals.
Stone Jug
Jug made of stoneware.
Stoned Horse
Stallion.
Stool Chair
Chair without arms.
Stool Pan
Pan for a *close barrel.
Stool Work
Tapestry work made on a stool.
Stoop
Post or pillar.
Stooper
A wedge used to tilt a barrel.
Stop
Small well bucket or milk pail.
Stopping Stick
Wooden block inserted into a shoe to hold its materials in place whilst the cobbler works on it.

Storax
A fragrant gum resin.
Store
1. The stock or tools of a tradesman.
2. Beasts such as pigs, kept for fattening.
Story
A painting or sculpture representing a historical subject.
Stot
1. A young ox or heifer. (Northern)
2. A horse, especially a plough horse. (Nth)
Stottrell
A small *stot or bullock.
Stouk Basket
Basket with a handle.
Stoup
1. Bucket or pail, usually wooden. (Northern)
2. Drinking cup, flagon or tankard; usually deep and narrow.
3. Post; gatepost. (Northern)
Stove
Grate or foot-warmer, burning charcoal.
Stover
Winter food for cattle.
Stow
A heated chamber or room.
Stowell
Stool.
Straik
A measure of timber.
Strait
Cloth of a narrow width, as opposed to *broad cloth.
Strake
A section of the metal rim of a cart wheel.
Strakine, Streke
Bundle of hemp, flax, etc. when dressed
Strang
Shaft. (Lan)
Straw Chair
Chair made of woven straw.
Straw Chip
Basket made of straw. (Dby)
Strawen
Made of straw.
Stress

Roof timber. (Dur)
Strickle
1. Wooden board covered with sand or emery; used to sharpen knives or sickles.
2. The implement by which a measure of grain was levelled to the rim of the measure; the amount so measured.
Strike
1. A measure of corn, from a half to four bushels, varying by locality; a measuring vessel of this capacity.
2. A bundle of hemp or flax.
String
Reins by which the ploughman controlled his oxen, or the rider his horse.
String of Land
*Selion: the basic unit of ploughing. (Sfk)
Stringer
Maker of bow strings.
Strip
Ornamental attire worn around the neck, chiefly by women.
Stripe
Any spoil or waste made on land by a tenant to the detriment of his land, e.g. making land barren by continual ploughing. (Hrt)
Strong Waters
Alcoholic spirits such as gin used as a beverage.
Stub
A short thick nail, especially an old horse-shoe nail, used for making stub-iron.
Stud
1. Large nail heads or bosses for harness decoration and/or protection.
2. An upright timber between principal posts in a timber-framed wall.
Stuff
1. Goods in general.
2. Worsted cloth without nap or pile; often dyed, patterned or printed; also used for any fabric.
Stump Bedstead
*Bedstead without posts and *tester.
Stun(d)
1. Half barrel or tub used in the dairy. (Sal)

2. Earthenware jar. (Sal)

Sture
*Steer.

Style Iron
Pointed instrument used for marking. (Ham)

Suck
The part of the plough which cuts underneath the slice of earth cut by the *culter.

Sucking Pig
Piglet: new-born or very young pig.

Succade, Suckett
Fruit preserved in sugar, either in syrup or candied.

Suffrage
Intercessory prayers; prayers for the soul of the departed.

Sugar Box, Chest
Chest or box for storing sugar.

Suit
A shroud or coffin.

Sull, Sullow
Plough. (South-West)

Sumach
A preparation derived from the sumach tree used in tanning and dyeing leather; also used medicinally.

Summoner
The official of an ecclesiastical court who summons people to attend.

Summer Tree
1. Principal beam of a floor.
2. One of the principal timbers of a waggon's bottom and sides.

Summerland
Land left fallow for a season to rest it.

Sumpter Cloth
Cloth placed under the saddle of a *sumpter horse; frequently ornamented.

Sumpter Horse
Horse used for carrying goods on its back: a pack horse.

Supercargo
The representative of the owner aboard a merchant ship.

Surces, Surcingle
Girth for a horse: the straps that keep the saddle or pack in its place.

Surety
Person offering a guarantee on behalf of someone else.

Surplice
1. A loose white vestment worn by clergy.
2. A labourer's smock frock. (Dor)

Surrogate
Deputy of an ecclesiastical judge; clergyman authorised to issue marriage licences on behalf of a bishop.

Surtout
Man's great coat or overcoat.

Suter
*Shooter.

Swaddle Bands
Narrow lengths of cloth wound round a new-born baby to prevent free movement.

Swage
1. An ornamental moulding, grooving, mount, or border on a candlestick, basin, etc., hence `swaged'
2. A blacksmith's tool for bending cold metal to the required shape; metal die or stamp for shaping wrought iron by hammering or pressure.

Swaler
Wholesale dealer in corn and provisions. (Lan)

Swarf
Iron filings or shavings; waste iron from a blacksmith.

Swath Bands
*Swaddle Bands.

Swathe Rake
A rake with wooden teeth and a long handle, used in hay-making to form swathes or rows.

Sway, Sway Pole
A crane or bar over a fire, from which pots could be hung.

Sweap
Pump handle.

Sweat Cloth
1. A cloth for horses.
2. Handkerchief.

Sweet Powder
Perfumed powder used as a cosmetic.

Sweet Water
A liquid perfume or scent.

Sweet Wort
In brewing, the wort before adding hops.

Sweetmeat
Confectionery, e.g. sugared nuts, fruit flavoured sugary sweets, etc.

Sweetwood
Timber from various West Indian trees.

Swift
Reel on which a skein of yarn is placed to be wound off onto the bobbins of a loom.

Swill
A large roughly made shallow basket.

Swill Tub
Tub for kitchen waste fed to swine.

Swine Form
A rough, wide, heavy form on which pigs were killed.

Swine Stock
Wooden collar for a pig, to prevent it pushing through hedges or straying. (Lin/Yks)

Swing Glass
Mirror suspended on pivots.

Swingle, Swingle Hand
Implement resembling a sword for beating and scraping flax or hemp to cleanse it of impurities; hence `swingling'.

Swingle Stock
1. Wooden box or trough into which cloth was placed to be beaten by the *swingle.
2. *Swingletree.

Swingletree
On a plough or cart, etc., the cross-bar pivoted in the middle, to which traces are attached, and which swings at the horse's or ox's heels.

Sylde
Bay or compartment.

Sylinge
*Sealed.

Sypers
Cypress tree, whose wood was used for making furniture.

Tabard
A sleeveless or short-sleeved coat.

Tabby
Silk taffeta, originally striped, but later applied to silks of uniform colour, waved or watered.

Tabernacle
Canopied recess or niche in a wall or pillar, perhaps ornate, to house the statue of a saint or other image.

Table
1. Payment for board and lodging.
2. *Table Board.

Table Basket
*Voider .

Table Board
The top or board of a trestle table, but not its *frame.

Table Carpet
Table cloth.

Table Chair
*Chair Table.

Table Form
Trestles.

Tableman
One of the pieces used in games played at table.

Tablet
1. A panel or slab, usually of wood, on which there is a picture or inscription.
2. A tile or slab used in roofing or flooring.
3. Loft. (Gls)

Tach, Tach Hook
Device for fastening clothes together, e.g. a clasp, buckle, eye and hook, etc.

Tack
1. A hanging shelf.
2. Clasp or board for a cheese container.
3. Pasture for cattle or horses hired out.

Tackle
Equipment, especially a horse's harness, etc.

Taffeta
In the 17th c., a thin plain woven glossy silk, usually with warp and weft of different colours.

Taffeta Sarcenet
Very fine *taffeta, used for linings.

Tag
An ornamental pendant; a tassel.

Tag Tail
Tagged: having a tail tipped with white or other distinctive colour.

Tagged
Out of condition or appearing to be unhealthy.

Tail Male
The entailment of an estate to male
heirs; each heir held an estate for life
only, and therefore could not dispose
of their family's long-term interest in it.

Tainte
A Spanish wine of low alcoholic
content.

Take
*Intake.

Talewood
Wood cut for fuel.

Tallage
A tax or aid imposed by feudal lords
upon their tenants; by the 16th c., a
municipal levy.

Tallet
1. Hay-loft with an open front, formed
by boarding joists over a stable.
2. *Tally.

Tallet Poles
Poles supporting a hay-loft.

Tallow
Hard animal fat used for making
candles, soap, dressing leather, etc.

Tallow Cake
A large ball of *tallow for use of a
*chandler (2).

Tally
A rod of wood, notched to indicate the
amounts of debts or repayments. They
were cleft along the notches, so that
both creditor and debtor could retain
one half as proof of the amount owed.

Talwood
Wood of a specific size cut for fuel.

Tamarine
A woollen cloth.

Tamarind
A tropical fruit valued for its medicinal
qualities.

Tambo Frame
A drum or frame on which linen was
stretched when being embroidered.
(Wor)

Tambour
Chain stitch embroidery worked
with a specially designed needle on a
tambour frame.

Tammy
A fine worsted cloth of good quality,
with a highly glazed finish; originally
made in Tamworth, Staffordshire.

Tan Garth
Tanning yard.

Tan Vat
Vat in which hides are steeped during
tanning.

Tang
Large girth used to fasten *panniers or
loads on a pack saddle. (Gls)

Tank, Tankard, Tankett
1. A tall drinking vessel with a handle
and lid.
2. A large wooden tub, perhaps made
of wooden staves and hooped, and
used in the dairy.

Tanner
One who tans hides to make leather.

Tap Borer
Tool for boring tap or bung-holes.

Tap Stone
Stone plug or stopper.

Tapestry
Decorated woven fabric used for wall
hangings, curtains, etc.

Taper
Large wax candle used for ecclesiastical
purposes, and often paid for by
executors to stand beside a coffin.

Tare
The seed of a vetch common in seed
corn, and which grows as a weed
amongst the corn.

Target
A light round shield or buckler.

Tass
A shallow cup. (Con)

Tassel
Teazle, used to raise the nap on cloth.

Taster
Small shallow cup, often silver, for
sampling wine.

Tavern
Cellar, usually a shop or workshop;
cupboard. Not necessarily underground.

Taw
A whip or lash.

Tawed
Made into white leather by steeping in
*alum and salt.

Tawer
A *tanner; one who prepares white

leather.

Tawny

A woollen cloth, light yellowish brown in colour (or the colour itself).

Tea Kettle Lamp

A small spirit lamp which could be placed under a tea kettle to keep it warm.

Team

1. Collective noun for a set or group of things.

2. Chains used with harness, by which horses or oxen pull their plough, cart, etc.

Tear

1. Fine, or delicate, used especially of flour and hemp.

2. Dressed hempen fibres for making into sheets.

Teasel

Plant with a burr-like head, used to raise the nap in finishing woollen cloth.

Teasing

Combing woven cloth to raise the nap.

Teath

*Cards.

Ted

The action of turning and spreading new mown hay to dry.

Teddar

Implement for tedding.

Teg

Yearling sheep before their first shearing.

Telle

*Till.

Temple, Temple Head

Device to keep cloth stretched on the loom during weaving.

Temps, Temse, Temser

A fine sieve, riddle, or *searce, used for *bolting flour, and often made of *hair; also used in brewing and the woollen trades.

Tend, Tene

Tine: the prong or tooth of a *harrow.

Tenement

Land holding, perhaps with a house; a dwelling place.

Tennet, Tenon Saw

Tenon or back saw; with thin blade,

small teeth, and a strong metal back.

Tent

A low-alcohol red Spanish wine, often used sacramentally.

Tent Bed

Small four-poster bed with an arched canopy and covered sides.

Tenter

Wooden frame on which cloth was hung to dry after milling; it had to dry evenly and without stretching or shrinking.

Tenter Hook

Hook or bent nail on a *tenter for holding the edges of the cloth in place; they are set closely together.

Terce

A measure for liquids; 42 gallons.

Tester

Flat canopy of a four-poster bed, made of wood and/or cloth, often carved, and supported on the bed posts or suspended from the ceiling.

Tew

Tool; implement.

Tew Iron

1. *Tuyere.

2. A blacksmith's long pincers, with which he draws iron from the forge.

Tewer

*Tuyere.

Tewtaw

Implement for breaking hemp or flax; a *hatchell. (West Midlands)

Thames

*Hames.

Thatch Rake

Implement with curved teeth used to straighten thatch when it is being laid on a roof.

Thatching Comb

A narrow strip of wood studded with nails, used to comb out short pieces of straw from the thatch.

Theal

A plank or board of wood; *deal.

Theave

Young female sheep which has not lambed.

Themell

Thimble.

Theorbo

A large lute with a double neck and two sets of tuning strings, the lower for the melody, the upper for base.

Thick-Set
Stout twilled cotton cloth.

Thill
Wooden shaft of a cart.

Thill Bell
The chain between the shaft-horse's collar and the tugs of the cart-shaft.

Thill Gear
Shaft harness.

Thill Hames
*Hames. (Lan)

Thin Drink
Small beer.

Third
The third part of a husband's personal and/or real property, given to his widow during her widowhood, especially in the Northern Province.

Thirdendeal
A third of a tun; the third part of anything.

Thixel
An *adze.

Thole
A pin used to fasten a shaft to a cart.

Thrall
A stand or frame for barrels or pots, on which they may be tilted.

Thrave
A measure of unthrashed corn, or of hay, rushes, etc., varying in different localities, but often two stooks of twelve sheaves each. (Northern)

Thread Edging, Thread Lace
Edging or lace made of linen or cotton thread, rather than silk.

Threshel
Flail for threshing grain.

Thrinter
Three years old.

Thripple
1. Chain tug leading from the collar of the horse to the shafts of the cart or *wain, etc. (Sal)
2. Movable sides of a cart, which could be extended to allow it to carry a greater load than would otherwise be possible.

Thriven

*Thrown.

Throck
The wooden beam on which the blade of a plough is mounted.

Throm Cloth
A coarse woollen cloth, with a rough, tufted surface.

Throw
A lathe on which wood is turned.

Thrower
Knife used for cleaning *laths and hurdles.

Thrown
1. Wood turned on a lathe, rather than `joined'.
2. Pots shaped on a potter's wheel.
3. Silk twisted into thread.

Thrum(b)
The loose ends or fringe of warp-threads left when the web has been cut off; hence cloth or cushions with tassels or fringes is `thrummed'. The waste was used as a coarse filling

Thwart Saw
Saw for cutting across timber; a cross-cut saw.

Tick, Ticking
Mattress case made of hard linen, and containing *flock or feathers, etc.; the cloth used for making the mattress case.

Tickney, Ticknall Ware
Coarse brown or black glazed earthenware, originating from Ticknall, Derbyshire.

Tie Wig
Wig with the hair gathered at the back and tied with ribbon.

Tierce
A measure of capacity, equal to a third of a pipe, or 42 gallons; a cask holding this amount.

Tiffany
Semi-transparent French silk or muslin fabric, used in veils.

Till
A small closed compartment in a larger box or *desk, to hold money or valuables.

Tiller Bow
In a cross-bow, the grooved wooden beam along which the arrow fits for

greater precision of aim.

Tilliwillie

Cloth made of *worsted. (Bdf)

Tilt

1. A covering, or awning of coarse cloth, for a wide variety of purposes, e.g. a waggon or cart, a tent, a saddle cloth, a boat, etc.

2. *Tilter.

Tilter

Wedges placed under barrels to keep them tilted, in order to empty them without stirring up the dregs.

Tilth

Cultivated ground, perhaps lying fallow.

Tilth Field

A ploughed field, ready for sowing.

Ting

The strap or *girse which fastens a *pannier to a saddle. (Dev)

Tingle Nail

The smallest type of nail; a tack.

Tinker

An itinerant craftsman who mends pots, pans, and other metal household utensils.

Tinker's Hammer

A light hammer used by a *tinker.

Tinker's Kettle

Pot or *cauldron made by a tinker.

Tinnen

Made of tin.

Tinsel

Rich and sparkling silk fabric, with gold and silver thread.

Tippet

Originally a strip of fur or cloth hanging from the sleeve or elbow; subsequently a short cape or cloak covering the neck and shoulders. A clergyman wore a black tippet over his surplice.

Tippler

Tavern keeper.

Tire

1. Iron rim of a cart-wheel.

2. A woman's head dress.

Tissue

Thin rich cloth, often interwoven with gold or silver.

Tithe

The tenth part of the produce of agriculture etc., to which parochial incumbents were legally entitled.

To-Fall

Lean to outbuilding; a *hovel.

Toasting Iron

1. *Salamander. (Gls)

2. Bread toaster.

3. Roasting iron for small pieces of meat, incorporating a small drip pan.

Tobacco Tongs

A light pair of tongs with a spring between its arms, used to pick up embers to light tobacco.

Tod

Measure of weight, usually 28lbs, but varying locally, used in the wool trade.

Toft

A homestead or *messuage; land on which a house has formerly stood.

Tog, Toggle

The two small handles of a scythe. (Dev)

Tog Withy

The *withies or bands which attached the *swingle tree to the head of the plough or cart, etc.

Toilinette

Fabric of cotton and silk, with a wool filling, used for men's waistcoats.

Token

A coin issued by a tradesman as a substitute for coins of the realm, when the latter were scarce.

Tone

*Tend.

Tongue Tree

The pole of a waggon or ox-cart. (Dev)

Tontine

A financial scheme by which subscribers to a fund each receive an annuity for their lives, increasing as their numbers are diminished by death, till the last survivor enjoys the whole income.

Top

Bundle of combed wool ready for spinning; slivers of wool fibre produced by the comb in manufacturing woollen cloth.

Torch

In a church, a processional candle;

often used for funerals.

Tortery, Tortree
Part of a horse's harness. (Sal)

Tottle
Vessel for boiling. (War)

Touch Box
A box for gunpowder; part of a
musketeer's equipment. It might also
be similar to a tinder-box, but using
touch-wood, which is a soft white
highly inflammable substance.

Tow
1. Either uncleaned wool, or the
shorter, coarser fibres of hemp or flax,
which have been separated by heckling
from the longer threads, and are ready
for spinning. Hence towen, made of
tow.
2. *Traces, chains or plough-lines.

Tow Comb
Comb for separating fibres of hemp or
flax.

Tow Wheel
Large spinning wheel for making yarn
of coarse *tow.

Towed Yarn
Flaxen or hempen yarn from which the
*tow has been removed.

Towel
1. Table napkin.
2. *Tuyere.

Towel Stick
A cudgel.

Town
1. A settlement; often means the
parish, although a single farmstead or
a hamlet might also be meant.
2. Coarse sheets made of flax or wool.

Traces
Ropes, chains or leather straps by
which a horse or ox's collar is linked to
the *swingletree.

Trag
*Drag (4). (Sts)

Trail Rake
Horse-drawn rake. (Ntt)

Trail Steed
Type of *sled cart. (Northern)

Train
Rope for dragging a plough or harrow.
(Nfk)

Train Oil

Oil from whale blubber, similar to
*tallow, used by clothiers and soap
makers.

Trained Band
Local militia force.

Trea
A sieve. (Sal)

Train Gown
Gown with a train at the rear, worn by
the upper classes on formal occasions;
the train was sometimes carried by a
page or train-bearer.

Tram
1. The shafts of a cart waggon or
wheel-barrow.
2. A wooden framework or stand on
which barrels and tubs could be stood.

Trammell
1. A long narrow fishing net with floats
and sinkers, consisting of two `walls' of
wide-mesh netting, between which is a
net of fine mesh.
2. A fowler's net.
3. A hobble for a horse, to prevent it
kicking or straying.
4. An instrument for drawing ellipses.
5. Rings, links, hooks or bar over a
fire-place, from which pots could be
hung at various heights.

Tran
*Trine

Trandle
*Dough kever.

Tranklement
*Hustlements. (Dby)

Transom
1. Mattress or bolster.
2. Cross-beam of stone or wood across
the top of a door or window.

Trap Reel
Used in conjunction with a spinning
wheel to measure yarn into hanks or
skeins. (Ess)

Trash
Household oddments not worth
valuing.

Tray
1. A wooden hurdle, often used for
folding sheep. (Lin; Yks)
2. Screen for sifting *malt from a kiln.
(Sal)

Treadle Wheel

Spinning wheel, which was operated from a sitting position by means of a treadle.

Tree

A stave or piece of wood, especially one that has been made into something, e.g. an *axletree, a *swingletree, a roof-tree, etc.

Tree Chain

Chain attached to a *tree, i.e. the wooden part of a plough.

Treen Ware

Wooden table ware such as bowls or *platters, usually *thrown rather than sawn, made out of single pieces of wood.

Treenails

Cylindrical pins of hard wood used to fasten timbers in ships together.

Tregar

Linen fabric from Treguier, Brittany.

Trencher

A thin, flat, wooden or pewter *platter from which food was eaten. It might be hollowed on both sides, so that meat could be eaten from one side, and a second course from the other. It often had a hole in the rim for salt, and might be square or round. Often made of sycamore. The name derives from the earliest form of plate, which was a thick slice of bread, in French `tranche'.

Trencher Salt

Large salt cellar.

Trendle

1. A large, oval, tub or trough, used for brewing or in the dairy.
2. A lump of wax. (Bdf)
3. A small wheeled truck or cart; see also *trundle. (Dev)

Trenket

1. Iron heel put on a shoe.
2. A shoe-maker's knife.

Trental

A set of thirty successive masses for the soul of the departed, perhaps all said on the same day.

Trepan

Surgical crown-saw, for cutting small pieces of bone from the skull.

Tress

The rope or chain etc., by which the *swingletree was connected to the collar of a draught animal.

Trestle

1. The detachable legs (always in pairs) which support a table board.
2. A long bench or form. (Dor)

Trimmer

A canopy.

Trindleware

*Treen.

Trine

Thirteen *felloes, or twenty-five spokes: the wheelwright's stock in trade.

Trippet, Trivet

Three-footed metal tripod for standing a pot over a fire; subsequently a metal bracket to hook on the bars of a grate.

Trochisk

Pastille or lozenge; a medical tablet.

Trolly

A kind of lace. (Dev)

Trose Bill

Hedger's hatchet. (Wor)

Trough

A narrow, open, v-shaped tank or vessel, made of wood, stone, metal or earthenware, often a fixture used for washing, kneading, brewing, etc., in the household.

Trouse

Close-fitting breeches or drawers, covering the buttocks and thighs, worn by men; knee breeches.

Trow

*Trough.

Trowel

A culinary ladle or slice.

Troy Weight

The standard unit of measurement for weighing precious metals; originally from Troyes, France.

Truckle

Castor wheel.

Truckle Bed

Low bedstead on castors or slides, without a head-board, which could be rolled or pushed under a *standing bedstead during the day time. Usually used by servants and children.

Trug

A shallow oblong wooden container,

perhaps a pan for milk, or a coal scuttle.

Trumpery
Items of little value, rubbish.

Trundle, Trunnill Bed
*Truckle Bed.

Truss
1. *Trouse.
2. A bundle of hay or straw.

Truss Bed
Portable bed which could be taken apart and trussed up for travelling, or perhaps a framed bed, using `truss' in its architectural sense.

Trusser
Strong heavy bench or table. (Dur)

Trussing Silk
Silk made into laces for lacing *doublet and *hose.

Try
Sieve or screen for sifting.

Tub
A wooden container, usually hooped and staved, capable of holding about half a barrel of water; if more it is a *vat; if less a *turnel.

Tuck
A slender pointed sword: a rapier.

Tucker
Person engaged in the fulling and dressing of cloth: a fuller or cloth-finisher.

Tucker's Handle
Handle fitted with teasles, for nap raising.

Tucker's Shears
Shears used in cloth finishing.

Tuft Mockado
*Mockado decorated with small tufts of wool.

Tug, Tugwithy
The *traces connecting the horse's collar to the *swingletree, or the rope or chain connecting the *swingletree to the head of the plough.

Tuition
Guardianship or upbringing.

Tuke
1. Canvas, or a finer fabric used to line garments.
2. *Tick. (Gls)

Tumbler

Drinking cup with a rounded bottom, so that it could not be put down until its contents had been drunk; often of silver or gold.

Tumbling Churn
Revolving barrel containing emery, in which castings were cleaned by friction. (Sfk)

Tumbrel
1. High-sided tipping cart on two wheels, often used to cart manure.
2. Frame for holding fodder in fold yards or the open field.
3. Counterpoise for raising a well bucket. (Lin)

Tun, Tunning
1. A large cask for ale, beer, wine, etc., holding 252 gallons, 2 *pipes, or 4 *hogsheads; the largest barrel in common use.
2. A *mashing fat or *gyle tun.
3. A cup or small drinking vessel.
4. *Tundish.

Tunbridge Ware
Small wooden objects lavishly decorated with parquetry patterns, made at Tunbridge Wells in the late 17th c.

Tundish
Wooden vessel with a tube at the base which fitted into the bung-hole of a cask or barrel, and thus formed a funnel.

Tunicle
Ecclesiastical vestment, worn by sub-deacons over the alb at celebrations of the eucharist.

Tunnel
1. A funnel.
2. A *turnel.
3. A net for catching partridges or water fowl. (Dur)

Tup
1. A ram. (Lan)
2. The head of a hammer. (Sal)

Tupping Hurdle
Hurdle to confine a ram. (i.e. a *tup)

Turf
Peat or cut turf used for fuel.

Turin
The nozzle of a pair of bellows.

Turkes

Precious stone from Persia of sky blue or light green colour, and almost opaque or translucent.

Turkey, Turkey Work
Cross-stitched woollen *carpet on a canvas backing, with a deep pile, woven from richly coloured yarn in the Turkish fashion, used as a covering for chairs, cushions, etc.

Turkey Colour
Azure.

Turkey Leather
Leather *tawed with oil.

Turling Bed
*Truckle Bed

Turmeric
Powder made from the aromatic root of an East Indian plant of the ginger family, used as a dye, a spice and medicinally.

Turn
1. Spinning wheel, spindle.
2. Churn. (Gls)
3. Winding gear for a well or grindstone. (Dby)

Turnbroach
Turnspit.

Turn Barrel
Winding apparatus at a mine.

Turn Up Bed
Bed that can be folded up when not in use.

Turncoat
1. A reversible coat.
2. Anything that changes its appearance or colour.

Turned
Furniture, especially chairs and tables, which has been turned on a lathe.

Turnel
1. A shallow oval tub or half-barrel, used for salting meat, kneading bread, making cheese, etc.
2. The windlass over a well.
3. A ring turning on a swivel, a terret, used on horse harness.

Turners Work
Furniture, etc., turned on a lathe.

Turnsole
Violet-blue or purple colouring matter, used in food and wine, and later as a pigment.

Turves
Turf or peat used as fuel.

Tutaw
*Tewtaw.

Tutor
Guardian.

Tuyere
The nozzle of a blacksmith's bellows, through which air is blasted to the base of his furnace or forge.

Twibill
Axe or mattock with two cutting edges.

Twiggen, Twigger
Basket work; made of twigs, wicker, rush, etc.

Twilight
1. Box containing toiletries. (Wor)
2. Rich covering for a dressing table. (Wor)

Twill, Twilly
A coarse linen fabric, in which the weft passes alternately over one warp thread and then under two or more threads, producing a lined effect; often used for bed coverings.

Twill Wheel
*Quill Torn.

Twilt
*Quilt.

Twin Doors
The entry doors of a house, at opposite ends of the cross passage.

Twinter
Cattle, sheep or colts of two years old.

Twist Lace
*Bobbin lace.

Tye
1. *Bed tick.
2. A green or common. (Sfk)

Tyre
*Strake

Ullage
The amount of wine or liquor by which a cask or bottle falls short of being full.

Umber
A brown earth used as a pigment; its colour.

Unbraked
Used of hemp: uncombed.

Underback
Vessel placed beneath a *mashing fat

to collect the raw *wort.

Unguent
Ointment or salve.

Untall Thread
*Outnal

Unwatered Camlet
Plain *camlet, i.e. `unwatered'.

Up Muck
Dung piled in heaps in the field ready for spreading. (Sts)

Upper Stock
The upper and wider part of the *hose.

Ure
1. Lead ore.
2. Ewer.

Use
Money `put to use' is earning interest.

Uster
*Worsted. (Dev)

Usclement
*Husslement.

Usquebaugh
Whisky.

Uting Vat
Vat for soaking or 'uting' barley before making *malt.

Utter
To offer goods for sale.

Uxor
Wife (Latin).

Vair
Squirrel fur.

Valance
Short curtain or border around the canopy or frame of a bedstead, or above a window; subsequently used to describe the border of any drapery.

Valencia
A mixed fabric with a woollen weft and silk or linen weft.

Valley
*Felloe.

Vamp
That part of the *hose which covers the foot; stocking or sock.

Vance Roof
Garret, attic, loft. (Nfk; Sfk)

Vandelas, Vandloes
A strong coarse canvas used for sails, made in Le Vendelais, Brittany.

Vantage
Profit, gain, advantage.

Vapour Bath
Form of Turkish bath used in the 18th c.

Vara
A Spanish linear measure, i.e. 33 inches.

Vat
A cask or tun, capable of holding more than half a barrel of liquid, used in brewing and cheese-making, etc.

Vellies
*Felloe.

Velour
*Velvet, or imitation velvet.

Velvet
A silk fabric with a short, dense smooth pile.

Ven Rake
Musk rake. (Dev)

Venetians
*Hose or knee breeches, introduced from Venice.

Venice Glass
Fine drinking glass or looking glass from Merano, close to Venice.

Venice Turpentine
Turpentine exuded from the bark of the white larch.

Verdigris
Copper salt used as a green pigment in dyeing, formed by the action of caustic acid on copper; also used medicinally.

Verdingal
*Farthingale.

Verdure
Rich tapestry decorated with representations of trees and shrubs; vivid green colour.

Verinas
Superior rolled tobacco, originally produced in Varinas, Venezuela.

Verjuice
The acid juice of crab apples (i.e. crab apple vinegar), or other sour fruit such as green walnuts and unripe grapes; kept in hogsheads, and much used in cooking and for dosing animals.

Vermilion
Red crystalline mercuric sulphide, used as a brilliant scarlet pigment, and in the manufacture of sealing wax.

Vessel
A worsted fabric formerly made in Suffolk.

Vessel Staves
The pieces of wood forming the sides of a barrel or vat.

Vestment
A garment worn by a priest during services and ceremonies.

Vetch
Leguminous plants such as clover and lucerne, used as cattle fodder; also used for bedding.

Vial Glass
A small, thin, glass bottle.

Vice
1. Screw stopper; the tap of a vessel.
2. Device or mechanical contrivance by which something is worked.
3. A spiral staircase. (Sfk)

Victualler
One who sells food and drink; an innkeeper.

Victuals at the Roof
Meat and other foodstuff hung from the roof or ceiling, inaccessible to rodents.

Vintner
A wine merchant.

Viol
A stringed musical instrument played with a bow; it had between five and seven strings.

Virgate
An English land measure, varying in size in different localities, but often thirty acres.

Virginal
A keyed musical instrument, set in a box or case without legs; similar to a *spinet.

Visor
That part of a helmet protecting the face, capable of being raised and lowered.

Vitry
Canvas cloth originally made in Vitré, Brittany.

Vizard
Mask with holes for eyes, nose and mouth, worn to conceal identity, to protect the skin from sun-light, and by ladies at the theatre.

Voider, Voiding Basket
1. A metal tray, basket or pail used for disposing of the scraps at meals, or for removing dirty plates etc., from the table.
2. A large wicker basket, usually used for dirty clothes.

Voiding Knife
A wooden utensil like a knife, for cleaning the remnants of food from a table.

Voler
*Roller.

Volmonger
Fellmonger: a dealer in hides, especially sheep-skins. (Con)

Vowess
A widow vowed to chastity for the rest of her life.

Wad
Woad: a blue dye-stuff.

Wadfat
Woad vat.

Wadmal
A coarse thick woollen material, used to line horse collars and for rough types of clothing.

Wafering Iron
1. Used for making crisp cakes and wafers, it consisted of two iron plates between which the paste was laid.
2. Rope or tie for securing a load on a cart.

Waggon
A strong, open, four-wheeled vehicle for carting hay, corn, etc., and furnished with *raves.

Waggon Pole
Shaft fitted to the forecarriage of a waggon, and attached to the collars of the draught animals.

Waggon Stock
Hub of a waggon wheel.

Wain
A *waggon used for agricultural purposes, for carrying heavy loads; most had four wheels, but the two wheeled variety was common in some areas, e.g. Cornwall, Lancashire, Yorkshire.

Wain Blade
Shaft of the *wain.
Wain Clout
*Clout .
Wainscot
Wooden panelling lining walls, usually
of oak; also applied to panelling on
furniture.
Waistcoat
A short garment worn on the upper
part of the body, usually beneath a
*gown, but so as to be seen; the earliest
waistcoats were often elaborate and
costly, and not necessarily without
sleeves.
Waiter
A salver or small tray; a dumb waiter.
Walker
Fuller; one who fulls cloth.
Walkers Earth
Fuller's earth, used to clean cloth.
Wall Bed
Bed fixed to a wall, sometimes with
doors; it could be folded up when not
in use.
Wallet
Bag for holding provisions or clothes
on a journey; a pedlar's pack.
Wampty
*Surces, surcingle.
Wanded
Wickerwork was made from wands,
i.e. young shoots of willow. Hence
`wanded'.
Want Staff
Moling spear, to catch moles.
Wantow, Wanty
Rope or *surces used to secure a pack
on a pack saddle, or a load on the back
of a horse.
War Saddle
Saddle for a cavalryman.
Warden Tree
A variety of pear.
Ware
1. Spring; hence `ware-corn', i.e.
spring corn. (Dur; Yks)
2. A collective term for the trade
goods of a merchant, pedlar,
tradesmen, etc.; merchandise.
Warming Pan
Shallow container of brass or copper,

with a long handle, filled with hot
embers, used to `iron' beds, and thus
warm them.
Warp
The threads that run lengthwise in
the loom, at right angles to the weft,
through which the latter must pass in
the process of weaving.
Warp Fat, Warping Vat
Vat or trough in which the weaver
places balls of yarn when running them
off for warping.
Warping Bar, Frame, Stock, Wough
The frame or bar on which the yarn
was wound to form a *warp before
transfer to the loom.
Warping Tree
Frame used in cloth-making.
Warren
A piece of land used for breeding
rabbits.
Wash
Brewery waste used as food for swine.
Washing Ball
A ball of soap.
Washing Maid
Wooden staff for pounding clothes
when washing them in a tub.
Washing Stock
Bench on which clothes were laid and
beaten with a bat; stand for a wash tub.
Washing Stone, Vat
Tub or stone trough for washing
clothes.
Wassail Board
A large board for mixing and storing
liquor, into which cups could be
dipped for drinking healths.
Watch and Ward
The duties of a night watchman.
Watch Bill
*Bill used by watchman, sometimes of
a military type; a *halberd.
Watchet
Pale blue cloth; the colour.
Water Bushel
Measure for goods such as coal, salt,
fruit, etc., sold on board ship. (Ham)
Water Candlestick
Vertical tub filled with water, holding a
floating candlestick.
Water Chaffer

A *chafer on which water could be heated.

Water Glover, Wet Glover
Maker of leather gloves.

Water Plate
Plate with a hollow bottom which can be filled with hot water to keep it warm, or perhaps a separate receptacle for hot water placed under a plate for the same purpose.

Waterchene
*Worsted material, perhaps dyed in several colours, with a watered or waved appearance.

Watered
Silk or other textiles with a wavy lustrous finish.

Watering Stone
Drinking trough for animals.

Wattle
Hurdle.

Way Tree
*Whipple Tree.

Weanling
An animal, usually a calf, being weaned, or just weaned.

Wearing Apparel, Clothes
Clothes, *apparel.

Wearing Band
Loose turn-over collar for the neck, which succeeded the ruff.

Weather Glass
Barometer or temperature gauge.

Weaving
Making textile fabric by crossing the *warp and the *weft.

Web
1. Piece of cloth in the process of weaving, or when it has just come off the loom.
2. Large piece of cloth, leather, metal, etc.

Webster
A weaver.

Wedset
A mortgage of land, or its conveyance in satisfaction of a debt, with provision for the debtor to recover it on payment of the debt or performance of some obligation.

Weeting Vat
*Uting Vat.

Weft
The thread that runs from side to side of the loom, at right angles to the *warp.

Weigh(ing) Back, Baulk, Beam
Transverse bar of a balance or set of scales, or perhaps the scales themselves.

Weights
Part of the mechanism of a jack used for turning spits in cooking.

Well Drag
Three-pronged drag for retrieving the bucket or things dropped in a well. (Dby; Ntt)

Well Throck
Windlass over a well. (Wil)

Welsh Hook
Bill-hook.

Welt
A narrow strip of material used to edge or border a garment, perhaps ornamentally.

Wemb(ing) Sheet
*Winnowing Cloth

Wemtell
Horse's belly band.

Wen
*Wain.

Went
A furlong of land; a portion of an open field separated from the rest of the field by some barrier, e.g. a road.

Wet Fish
Fresh fish, not dried.

Wet Larder
Larder for storing moist or liquid provisions.

Wether
A male sheep, especially a castrated ram.

Wether Hog
Male sheep before its first shearing.

Wey
Standard of dry goods weight; varying in amount according to the commodity being weighed.

Wharl
*Quarrel.

Whearne
*Quern.

Wheat Manchet

Loaf or roll of white bread; muffin; hot cake, etc.

Wheel
Usually a spinning wheel or *turn.

Whelff
*Felloe. (Lin; Yks)

Whepe
A pruning knife. (War)

Wherry
A large four wheeled cart without sides.

Which, Whitch
1. A bin or tub made of split planks of oak wedged and pegged together; a chest, coffer or hutch. Used for storing meal, flour, etc.
2. A sieve or wicker strainer. (Wor)
3. Salt.

Whichhouse
Place for drying brine for salt. (Chs)

Whiff
*Coif. (Dev)

Whin
Gorse or furze.

Whip Saw
1. Frame saw with a narrow blade for curved work.
2. A long, narrow, two-man saw used in a saw pit.

Whip Whang
A long thin strip of leather used for the lash of a whip. (Lin; Yks)

Whipcord
Thin, but tough, hempen cord, used for making whips.

Whippence
The fore-carriage of a plough or harrows. (Wil)

Whipple Tree, Whipping Tree
A free-swinging piece of wood to which the *traces of a plough, harrow, etc. were attached; a *swingletree.

Whisk
1. A brush made from leather, twigs, hair, etc., bound together on a stick.
2. A cape or short cloak. (War)

White Candlestick
Made of silver.

White Cloth
Undyed cloth.

White Coal
Wood cut into small pieces, dried in a kiln, and turned into charcoal for smelting.

White Grain
Wheat, barley, and oats, rather than peas and beans.

White House
Dairy.

White Latten
Tinplate.

White Lead
Compound of lead carbonate and hydrated oxide of lead, used as a white pigment.

White Leather
Horse skin cured with lime; used for parchment and for strong laces, being hard and tough.

White Meat
Dairy produce.

White Metal
Various alloys coloured light grey.

White Money
Silver coin.

White Plate
Enamelled tin-plate.

White Salt
Salt for household use.

White Silver
Silver ware chased or roughened, as opposed to burnished.

White Smith
Smith who finished off goods begun by other smiths, e.g. attaching the haft to an axe head, fitting the pieces of a gun together, etc.

White Ware
White earthenware of good quality.

White Work
Cut and slashed lace.

Whitening
Crushed chalk, used to whiten floors or walls. (Wil)

Whitsull
*Whitemeat. (Dev)

Whittawer
A saddler or glover: one who worked in white leather.

Whiting
Bleaching.

Whittle
1. A baby's flannel petticoat; a shawl for women, especially nursing mothers. (South West)

2. A cloak.

3. A large knife; a carving knife or butchers knife. (Northern)

Whye
*Quy. (Dur, Yks)

Wick
An enclosed piece of land, a close, a dwelling place, hamlet, village or dairy farm.

Wick Yarn
Yarn used as a wick in candles, lamps, or tapers.

Wicker
Pliable twigs, usually willow, used for basket-making.

Wicket
A small door or gate beside a larger one, for use when the latter is closed; also any small gate for pedestrians.

Widge Beast
A horse. (Dev)

Wig Block
Rounded block on which a wig was stored when not in use.

Wimble
1. A gimlet, *auger, or brace, for boring holes.
2. A hay trusser's tool for twisting and plaiting ropes of straw or hay.

Winding
Rod or withy for making and repairing a wall or other building work. (Sts)

Winding Blade
Spindle for winding thread or yarn.

Wind(ing) Cloth, Sheet
1. *Winnowing Cloth.
2. Shroud in which a body is wrapped for burial.

Windlass
Hand operated winding drum, for raising and lowering masts, raising minerals from a pit, raising buckets from a well, etc.

Windle
1. A winnowing basket.
2. *Windle Blade.
3. *Windlass.

Windle Blade
Spindle for winding a skein of yarn into a ball.

Window
*Window Leaf.

Window Board
A shutter.

Window Cloth
1. Cloth used in place of glass for a window.
2. *Winnowing cloth.

Window Grate
Framework or bar preventing entry through the window.

Window Leaf, Leam
Removable window, including both glass and frame.

Window Lid
*Lid.

Window Sheet
*Window Cloth.

Windsor Chair
Chair with a solid seat and semi-circular back, and sometimes with arms. The back and legs are spindles

Wing
Iron side piece of a grate.

Wingle
*Windle Blade.

Winnowing Cloth, Sheet
Winnowing was the process of separating the grain from the chaff after threshing. The grain was sieved or screened in the wind (either natural or created by a winnowing fan). The chaff blew away, but the grain fell on the winnowing sheet.

Winter Corn
Wheat or rye, sown in the autumn.

Wiper
Handkerchief.

Wisket
A strong osier bucket, used in the garden, for animal fodder, and for various other purposes. It had a hole at each end for carrying, rather than a handle.

Withy
Willow tree; also applied to its branches, which are very flexible, and were used extensively in basket making, the seats of chairs, for tying or binding, etc.

Witney
A heavy woollen cloth with a nap, made in Witney (Oxf), and used for blankets.

Woad
A blue vegetable dye.
Woad Vat
Vat in which woad was fermented and prepared for use as a dye, or in which cloth was dyed using woad.
Womb
The belly piece of a hide used in shoe-making.
Wombing Sheet
*Winnowing Cloth.
Womble
*Wimble .
Wong
Unenclosed land in the open field: a group of *selions or strips. (Lin)
Wood Coal
Charcoal obtained from wood.
Wood Knife
Huntsman's dagger, for cutting up game or as a weapon.
Woodwax
Dyer's greenwood: *genista tinctoria.*
Woodwose
A wild man of the woods, especially in visual art.
Wool Card
*Card.
Wool Comb
*Comb.
Wool Driver
One who buys wool from the producer to sell to the clothmaker.
Wool Fell
Sheepskin with the fleece still on it.
Wool Wheel
A spinning wheel for wool.
Woolsey
Woolly, woollen.
Workhouse
Workshop where a trade or craft was carried on; not usually a `workhouse' in the poor law sense - they mostly came in the 19th century.
Worm
Screw of a screw press.
Worm Seed
Seed of a Levantine plant used medicinally to kill intestinal worms.
Worm Tub
Tub used in distilling.
Worsted

A closely twisted yarn of long staple wool, which has been combed rather than carded to make the fibres lie parallel to each other; the fabric made from this yarn. Originally made in Worstead, Norfolk.
Wort
The infusion of *malt which becomes beer after fermentation; unfermented beer.
Wort Fat, Store, Trough, Tub
Vat etc., in which *malt is fermented in beer-making.
Wort Pan
Pan used for drawing off the *wort from the *mashing fat in the brewing process.
Worthing
Manure; dung. (Lan)
Wrathe
*Rave. (Yks)
Wring
A press, e.g. a *cheese press, *cider press.
Writing
A legal document, e.g. a *bill, *obligation, deed, etc.
Writing Obligatorie
*Obligation.
Wrought
Worked, woven, knitted, embroidered, decorated, ornamented, hand-carved, shaped, fashioned, etc.
Wrystes
The part of the plough which turns up the earth in furrows. (Bdf)
Wynding Sheet, Wynnying Sheett, Wynow Cloth, Wynsheate
*Winnowing Cloth.
Wyrgen
A very coarse canvas used for baskets. (Oxf)

Yard Arm
A spar on a ship's mast.
Yard Wand
Measuring rod, three feet long.
Yardland
The size of a holding in the open fields which might be made up of several strips in various different places; generally 30 acres, but varying by

locality. (Midlands)

Yarn

Spun fibre of wool, flax, silk, etc., used for weaving or knitting.

Yarn Blade

*Windle Blade.

Yate, Yeate

Gate.

Year Tub

Tub with `ears' i.e. handles. (Dev)

Yearn Ware

Earthenware.

Yeeling, Yelding, Yeln

*Gyle.

Yeld

Animals that are barren.

Yellow Brass

A paler shade of the alloy, made by varying the proportion of zinc to copper.

Yellow Griete

A type of earthenware pottery. (Chs)

Yeo

Ewe.

Yeoman

Substantial tenant farmer or freeholder.

Yetling

A small iron pot with three feet and a bow handle. (Lin; Yks)

Yewing

Suckling. (Yks)

Yoke

1. A curved wooden bar placed over the shoulders of two horses or oxen, to harness them together; they are usually fitted with *ox bows, and there is a central ring or hook for attachment of the *chain or *trace by which their load is drawn.

2. A wooden bar, shaped for the shoulders, from each end of which a bucket is hung, used for ease of carrying.

Yorkshire

Thick, coarse cloth made in Yorkshire.

Yoting Trough

Trough used for steeping barley in water for malting.

Yrne

Iron.